The
POWER
SEAT

The
POWER
SEAT

your interview. your life. your success.

CHRISTINA NEPSTAD

"Life is an interview: Be prepared with a successful strategy."

PINECREEK PUBLISHING

Copyright ©2016 by Pinecreek Publishing.
All rights reserved.
Cover Design by Tyler Dutton
www.ThePowerSeat.com

ISBN 978-0-692-56235-2

Table of Contents

Smile Inside

Destiny is funny,
Yet much like putty.
We all have a choice,
Like a silent voice.
Lying so low,
Going with the flow.
Take a stand,
Regardless of reprimand.
Within our imaginations,
Began life's creations.
So make a decision,
And create a vision.
When you can visualize,
Then you will realize,
Your visualization can become
Your destination.
Finally set free,

THE SMILE INSIDE OF ME!

– Written by Dawn B., client of The Power Seat program.

Acknowledgments

Sequoia – A treasured and loyal assistant. Thank you for sharing your story!

Dr. Savitha Siddappa – Not only an amazing dentist, but a valued friend and mentor. Thank you!

Dawn "Patrol" – Thank you for the beautiful poem. You are a champion.

Thank you Alex Padua for your insight and direction for The Power Seat.

To my clients, all of whom have helped develop the principles of the Power Seat, thank you!

"Sheldon" – Working with you has challenged me to be better. You are inspiring and brilliant. I'm grateful to call you a friend and partner.

Moana – Thank you for all you do as a Power Seat team member. Your light shines with positivity. "Mahalo!"

Jess, Hope and Heath – Your sacrifice, love, and unwavering support will be forever appreciated. I dedicate The Power Seat to you.

Praise for The Power Seat

"Christina is my "go-to" coach when it comes to learning how to take the Power Seat. Her coaching is without a doubt the best in the business. I have been in the entertainment industry since I was 16, yet it's because of the principles I learned from her program that I am now a full-fledged producer and manager with The Alternative at the age of 28."

– Jamie Gruttemeyer

"The Power Seat formula has forever changed the way I think about and express myself. It worked for me and it can work for you too!"

– Sequoia Foster

"Experiencing The Power Seat program firsthand was exhilarating and powerful. It's a meaningful process that pokes at one's conscience and consciousness…it left me feeling uplifted and empowered."

– Moana Walker

"I am currently working on my PhD in Education and what Christina's program has taught me really translates to much of what I am doing academically and professionally. My time with her was an incredible investment! I recommend anyone to work with her and everyone to pick up her book!"

– Yasamine Bolourian

"How marvelously conceived is The Power Seat program. Christina will advance your conviction that effective interviewing is not only possible—it is certain. A must for any woman who dreads sitting before a CEO, or board, navigating that all important interview session upon which her success depends!"

– Donna Fontaine

"I believe the skills and principles of The Power Seat will benefit all professionals."

– Maureen Tucker

"The Power Seat principles have empowered me to become the best version of myself and have taught me how to put my best foot forward in every interview situation. Regardless of one's vocation or personal goals, I highly recommend reading Christina's book and applying her methods in order to be successful in everyday life."

– Kara Smoot

"I took part in this program as a young adult to better myself and my professional career. Now as a mother of two daughters, the tools I have kept allow me to be a better mother and leader. I'm indebted to Christina for instilling an inner strength that I never knew I had."

– Nicole Torres

"Christina has empowered me with invaluable insight on how the Power Seat is something that comes from within. We all have it, but she helps you activate it! And when you find it, it's truly the best SEAT in the house."

– Joli Lallo

"As a young woman standing at the edge of "the real world," life often can feel out of control. With the tools I have taken from Christina's Power Seat method, I have a sense of confidence in every situation life throws my way."

– Carley Ryckman

"Christina is a powerful inspiration, making an extraordinary difference in the lives of women. She embraces the art of interviewing, transforming lives and allowing ones confidence to grow beyond measure and thus their lives change forever."

– Sandy Bryan

"When it comes to my life, I have always had a difficult time dealing with change. When I graduated from college, I had a really tough time transitioning from a college student to a young adult. Then I came to Christina to train for a state competition and my life was changed forever.

I will be completely honest: The Power Seat program is not for the lighthearted. It was emotionally intense, tough to swallow—and exactly what I needed. Through Christina's program, I was finally able to not only discover who I am, but to truly embrace who I am—everything about myself, good and bad—the 80 and the 20! I found true balance in myself and learned how to reflect that balance in social situations, job interviews, and public speaking events. Now 27, I am a professional singer and am training in a career in development for theatre companies. To this day, one of the biggest compliments I receive is how natural I appear speaking publicly and how eloquent and personable I am when interacting in a social environment or in that everyday interview. Whenever I receive these compliments, I think of Christina—and The Power Seat."

– Kayla Bailey

"The Power Seat isn't about changing who you are—it's about embracing the strength that is already inside of you. I'm forever grateful that the teachings from her program continue to empower me every day."

– Jane Kennedy

"The Power Seat program has taught me to be myself in a very confident way in any interview situation. I have learned how to take The Power Seat and I have become my own best friend."

– Cassandra Bateman

"Through The Power Seat program I discovered my strengths, and most importantly, my voice."

– Megan Wisler

"Knowing who you are is a special gift that not many people have. This program helped me find exactly who I was and that's something I'll never take for granted. I really grasped an understanding that an interview is simply an **inner-view** of you and people just want to know who you are. I've received awards because of my communication skills learned through this program and I know it will help me reach success in my future"

– Hayley Hunt

"The POWER SEAT is a must-read for women everywhere- it will give you the tools to convey your personal experience, education and skills making you the ONLY choice!"

– Barbara Bayer Coulter

"Twenty-four years ago I was the first client to walk through the doors of what was then, **The Smile Inside program**. I worked with Christina and accomplished my goal of becoming Miss Colorado Teen USA and winning top interview! How exciting to think I was the first of many to benefit from Christina's teachings."

– Brandi Ginn

"The *Power Seat* program is powerful, thought provoking and life changing. Christina provided deep insight into my personal and professional life. Her highly effective interview program made me successful starting in pageants, to a high-level corporate job and now as Founder of MommyBistro.com. The right program can make all the difference and this is it!"

– Jessica Gesell, Mommy Bistro

Introduction

As a young girl, I remember being terrified by my own words. The simplest conversations left me drenched in anxiety and wanting to drown myself in the nearest vat of Ben & Jerry's ice cream. I was uncomfortable communicating. Of course, I was deathly afraid of interviews. It didn't help that I was consumed with what others thought of me, which only left me more confused as to what I thought of myself.

When I think back on those times, I am convinced my fear and anxiety came from not having a clear grasp on who I was. This made me vulnerable, weak, and incredibly insecure. No wonder I never got the job, opportunity, or even the boyfriend I had hoped for.

The truth is simple. How well you know yourself will determine the way you communicate. How you communicate will shape every aspect of your life. You've heard the saying, "You can't sell what you don't know." That being said, how effective can you really be if you have not majored and minored in yourself first?

The Power Seat program will help you understand and appreciate the unique connection between self-awareness and a game-changing communication style. Whether you're a college graduate looking for your first job, a busy mom ready to re-enter the workplace, an accomplished individual in pursuit of a career change, or a contestant in a beauty contest, this program will help give you the confidence you need to successfully handle your interview.

In all likelihood, you're reading this book because you are interested in what the Power Seat can do for you. Possibly, you have an interview in the near future. Congratulations!

I'm proud of you for being willing to take a chance and put yourself out there for the sake of pursuing a goal or dream. I am excited for you to take the same journey that led me to find my true communicative powers. This program is exactly what you need to achieve your goal and breathe new life into your dreams.

THE POWER SEAT DIFFERENCE

Before we begin, let me ask you a question: "How well do you know yourself?" This is the key to unlocking what I call the *Power Seat Difference*.

I'm sure you want to have the most effective, powerful, and confident interview experience possible. But what's going to set you apart from the others competing for the job? What's going to give you the ability to penetrate, persuade, inspire, and leave them wanting more? How will you convince the interviewer to appreciate your unique set of strengths? How well will you answer questions like:

- "What can you offer this company?"

- "How have you learned from a mistake you've made in your past?"

- "Why would others want to follow your leadership?"

- "What aspects of your personality fit best with this particular opportunity?"

- "Why do you want this job?"

- "What are your greatest professional strengths?"

The first question I ask my clients is, "How have you prepared for your interviews in the past?"

Most will say they have been reviewing their accomplishments, brushing up on current events, studying facts about the employer, and practicing how to answer random questions.

Indeed, it is a good idea to know your facts and have relevant information about the company or person with whom you'll be speaking. However, you must understand one crucial point: An interview has more to do with you than with anyone else in the room. This is because an interview is actually an "inner-view" of you!

This is the Power Seat difference. It's quite a change from the typical interview advice you often find. That's what makes it so eye-opening and effective.

Today, most people prepare for an interview with a performance-based approach. They employ a calculated strategy dependent upon prepared responses. This kind of preparation involves memorization and a "fake it till you make it" attitude. Unfortunately, it also encourages the interviewee to say whatever she thinks will please the interviewer. This is a slippery slope where most tend to lose their balance. If you are offered the job, it's likely to be a poor fit with your true strengths and abilities.

A false presentation is always a compromise of integrity. This flawed approach can lead to an automatic job dismissal if you were hired on a false premise.

Perhaps most importantly, a false presentation is counterproductive to the goal of representing you as you really are. You are a unique and valuable individual. You deserve to find a job that is a good fit. You deserve a job where you'll be appreciated for who you are.

It can be tempting to try to say all the right things to get the job, but trying to anticipate every question with a "perfectly" prepared response is a waste of your talents and time. Your next interview will be mostly about you, guaranteed.

According to The Power Seat, you should be the one with all the power. After all, you determine what they hear. Let's face it—most of the time we feel vulnerable going into an interview setting. If we don't have a Power Seat, then most likely we are stuck in the hot seat. That is a scary place to be! Therefore, we will work together through a groundbreaking program that will provide graphs, charts, questionnaires, practical examples, and daily activities to keep you inspired and on point.

Never forget that your individuality is what separates you in a unique way. There is no substitute for that. The road you must take to capture and define what that is can get rocky, dirty, and downright confronting, but I promise it's worth it! No matter where you are in your life, with this approach, you'll be sure to deliver an authentically powerful offering of yourself with every interview experience. Time to get moving and get you in that Power Seat!

Before you get started on your Power Seat journey, answer these interview questions to the best of your ability. As you get to the end of the book you will have an opportunity to answer the same questions, but with the knowledge of your Power Seat training.

"What can you offer this company?"

_____

"How have you learned from a mistake you've made in your past?"

_____

"Why would others want to follow your leadership?"

_____

"What aspects of your personality fit best with this particular opportunity?"

_____

"Why do you want this job?"

_____

"What are your greatest professional strengths?"

_____

These answers are a good place to start and an excellent example of how well you have prepared for your typical interview. Please mark this page because we will be revisiting these answers after you have completed this book.

Chapter 1:
What Is an Interview?

I walked on the stage with perfect posture and a dress that would stop traffic.

At 24, I was boldly vying for the Miss USA title. It was time for my interview. I had studied hundreds of sample questions and perfected my responses. Being the last contestant in the semifinals to go on, I had been glued to the TV monitor and certain from what I heard that I had rehearsed all the possibilities perfectly. With all my preparation, I assumed I was ready to take home the crown.

Each of the top ten contestants before me had answered a question. Mine was a two-parter: "Have you always been this beautiful?" and "I understand that you had a weight problem when you were younger. How did you lose the weight?"

I won't sugarcoat it. I hadn't expected to be asked about my weight problem or anything I hadn't already rehearsed. I'd worked hard to drop those excess pounds, but my weight was still a source of tremendous insecurity and something I didn't want to share on national television. In front of the audience, I wanted to appear confident and in control.

Since I was caught off guard by the question about my weight, and since I hadn't prepared for this interview by learning my own "inner-view," my answer was powerless. I stumbled, sputtered, and bumbled my way through the rest of the pageant interview.

My answer was weak, hollow, and ineffective, leaving me powerless and defined by my failure. Worse yet, my feelings of total inadequacy were eager to help me believe I was a victim. I had the ammunition I needed to blame someone other than myself for that awful dialogue exchange. I couldn't wait to claim I was blackballed, set up, victimized, and embarrassed.

The facts would eventually catch up with me in what would be a humbling learning experience. One day, I attended the wedding of a friend. Dick Clark, the famous radio and television personality who had served as the Miss USA pageant emcee and the one who asked the question that had so ruffled me, was also a guest. The moment I saw him at the reception, my feelings took over again. Since the night of my disastrous pageant interview, I had blamed him for asking such a random question and single-handedly ruining my chance at taking home the crown.

In my mind, this was my chance to expose him and justify my feelings. I swallowed my gum, cleared my throat, and calmly approached him. I asked Dick how he had found out about my struggle with weight. I demanded to know why he would be so cruel as to ask me about it on national TV. Didn't he realize that asking a young woman about such a sensitive issue was the equivalent of setting her up for public humiliation? Where was his sense of compassion?

Dick seemed hesitant to respond. I was sure he was gathering the courage to come clean and finally give me the apology I believed I deserved. Instead, he told me his assistant had overheard me talking to the other contestants about my struggle with my weight. As part of the discussion, I had mentioned that I had changed my diet and exercise habits to lose the excess weight and improve my overall health.

His assistant had suggested the question because she thought my story was inspiring. Knowing that many of the pageant viewers would be experiencing similar struggles, Dick agreed.

It turned out that Dick wasn't being malicious at all. He honestly believed other women could benefit from what I had to say.

Dick's decision to ask me that question was an opportunity I had missed because I let my feelings be interpreted as facts. All this time, I believed what my feelings told me to believe. I never tried to prove or disprove the accuracy of how I felt. I just ran with my feelings because they provided a convenient way to justify my own powerless interview.

I'm embarrassed to admit that I wasted a great deal of time reliving that night on the pageant stage. Can you imagine what my life would have been like if I had never run into Dick Clark at that wedding? I would probably still believe the lies of my feelings!

To make matters worse, I missed the chance to demonstrate true leadership and to inspire those around me. If I would have recognized the question for what it was, I may very well have been able to use my position to motivate young women across the country to make healthier lifestyle choices. Losing weight is a difficult process, and helping others to reach their goals would have given me great personal satisfaction.

When I imagine being back on that stage, I think about how my interview would have gone had I been in the Power Seat and equipped with the appropriate knowledge to effectively speak from my strengths. Here's how I imagine I would have answered that tricky question:

Dick Clark: "Miss California, have you always been this beautiful?"

Me: "Mr. Clark, beauty is complicated. Perhaps you have heard the saying, 'Pretty is a gift, beauty is what you do with it.' It wasn't until I understood the meaning of this expression that I became beautiful to myself."

Dick Clark: "I understand that you had a weight problem when you were younger. How did you lose the weight?"

Me: "As a young girl, I used food to help me deal with stress. I didn't understand the purpose of food or the effects it could have on my body. As I became educated in nutrition, I also learned to respect myself and my body. I hope I can encourage anyone out there struggling with similar issues to know that they have what it takes to make a positive change."

EVERYDAY INTERVIEWS

Whether we're competing in a pageant or trying to snag our dream job, the formal interview is often what brings to light our insecurities and uncertainties. The thought of taking part in a dialogue that will be judged, examined, cross-examined, interrogated, and assessed based upon what you say can be terrifying.

In order to understand the concept of an interview, we must consider it on a grander scale than the formal setting. In reality, we are interviewing constantly. Think about the last time you stopped to greet someone you hadn't seen in quite some time. Within moments, you were likely asked questions such as,

- "How are you?"
- "What have you been doing?"
- "Where are you working?"
- "Where are you going to school?"
- "How are your children?"

Maybe you've been interested in trying to get on the school board and inquiring minds want to know:

- "Why does this position interest you?"
- "What do you think is the biggest issue facing our school?"
- "What are you hoping to change if you win the election?"
- "Why are you the one who can make a difference?"

Dating is another area in which we're always interviewing potential prospects. The dating interview has questions like,

- "What do you want to do with your life?"
- "Do you want kids? If so, how many?"
- "Why did your last relationship fail?"
- "What are you looking for now?"

Sometimes the casual interview is a simple endeavor, but it might become more complicated. Keep in mind that any interview is an "inner-view" of you. Most of us think we do fine in these daily informal interviews. It's true that we enter in and out of them unscathed for the most part. But, how often are you accurately reflecting what you really know about who you are? How often are you missing the chance to add real value or influence to a conversation?

I'm going to take a moment to make a bold statement. Most of us pretty much stink at the casual everyday interview. We don't know ourselves well enough to be influenced by the knowledge we possess. We tend to put our efforts into achieving culturally-driven dialogue.

If our thoughts are not based on our knowledge, we are being repeatedly misidentified. Your thoughts show up in your words. Your words define you as a person, regardless of the particular situation you find yourself in.

PREPARING TO TAKE THE POWER SEAT

Imagine if all your interviews, both formal and informal, originated from a place of expert knowledge. How exciting would it be to supply your listener with the best of who you are every time? Instead of approaching an interview with nervousness and anxiety, you'd be ready to confidently share your views and show the world what you have to offer.

Years ago, I had a client who couldn't visualize herself being interviewed from such a position of power. Because of her anxiety, she assumed the most powerful chair in the room belonged to the one asking the questions.

This is simply not true! You are in the Power Seat because you are the expert on the subject of YOU! As an interviewee, you determine what people hear. This role means that you are the one with the power. You are in the Power Seat. Even if you desperately need to land the job because you're only a few weeks away from being evicted from your apartment, keep in mind that you've already beaten out multiple applicants by having landed the interview. The interviewer wants nothing more than to believe in your skills and abilities. He or she wants to hear what you have to say. As an interviewee, there are two reasons you have power: You are the expert on yourself, and you determine what the interviewer hears.

The Power Seat symbol most likely makes you think of presidents, queens, leaders, celebrities, or important officials. We believe such a seat is reserved for people who know what they're talking about. They are experts, specialists, authority figures, connoisseurs, or maestros. We expect them to demonstrate confidence, leadership, influence, skill, and expertise. We assume they have special qualities that the rest of us mere mortals could only dream of possessing. In our minds, they're put on a pedestal by nature of their position.

In reality, a lot of people only appear powerful. Just because someone is in a seat of power does not mean they're in the Power Seat. The world is full of people who have ended up in positions of power without demonstrating true leadership skills. Eventually, most fall from grace.

You can't take the Power Seat before you're ready, no matter what title you have listed on your business cards. Knowing how to offer the best of yourself for the benefit of others is a critical prerequisite to the Power Seat.

Sometimes it's hard to determine what true power is. Power is often abused and misinterpreted. The following chart should help you have a better understanding of what it looks and sounds like to possess the Power Seat:

Real Power IS	Real Power IS NOT
• Born from a place deep within	• Acquired
• Able to stand alone in confidence	• Excuses
• Individual, unique, and personal	• Selfish or self-seeking
• Honorable and understated	• Proud or loud
• Respectable	• Forced
• An offering	• A taking
• Available to all who understand it	• Reserved for the privileged

To be in the Power Seat, you must have faith in your abilities and understand how to use them to perform the task at hand. Otherwise, you're setting yourself up for failure.

To prepare yourself, you need to have a solid understanding of yourself. But remember, it takes time to equip yourself with the inner knowledge that produces unforgettable and unmatchable interviews. Give yourself the time and space to peel the onion, to learn about all those complex and fascinating layers down deep.

While this program may be relatively quick, your transformation will not be instant. As you study yourself, you will also teach yourself. Then, it's time to practice what you've learned until you're ready to blow your audience away.

POINTS TO REMEMBER

- Interviews aren't just a part of the job application process. We're interviewing every day, both formally and informally. For example, going on a date could be considered a type of informal interview.

- In an interview, the Power Seat belongs to you. The interviewer has invited you to speak, thus demonstrating an interest in what you have to say. By providing an honest dialogue, you're showing your strength.

- To prepare yourself for a successful interview, you need to have a solid understanding of both your strengths and weaknesses. Remember, an interview is an "inner-view" of you!

- Changing your interview style won't happen overnight. The Power Seat program will introduce you to key concepts, but you'll need to practice them each day until you're ready to approach every interview with complete confidence.

- The Power Seat is only powerful because of the woman in it. Embrace your inner power, and success will come naturally.

Activity: The Power of Identification

"Truth is powerful and it prevails." – Sojourner Truth

My clients are eager to figure out what to say in order to get the job. They want to stand out and be the obvious choice. Most are qualified professionals and good conversationalists with lots of friends. However, they are missing something vital for success: They don't have a grasp on their power.

My efforts to teach women how to ace their interviews have been successful because of the power of identification and imagery. It is a similar concept to a woman in labor who is directed from the beginning of her birthing classes to identify with a focal point. The Power Seat is a reminder to stay true to what put you there in the first place. This focal point helps to keep your mind on the purpose.

Once the Power Seat and its image are in your mind, the concept takes on a profound meaning. Suddenly you can see, touch, and imagine yourself in that place of power.

Let's take a closer look at what being in the Power Seat involves.

Describe your last formal interview:

_____

_____

_____

_____

Describe your last casual interview:

_____

_____

_____

_____

How did you feel after both of these interviews? At what point did you experience anxiety or uncertainty?

_____

_____

_____

_____

WHAT IS AN INTERVIEW?

Name three people you believe are in positions of power:

1. _____

2. _____

3. _____

What qualities do these people reflect that let you know they are in the Power Seat?

_____

_____

_____

_____

Chapter 2:
The POWER of 80/20

"Knowledge is Power." – Francis Bacon

Most of us think we know who we are. In fact, we are sure of it! In reality, most of us haven't majored and minored in ourselves at all. Recently, a friend sent out a general email asking for others to help identify her areas of strength and weakness. She was hoping to gain some insight on herself but forgot to consider that any feedback would be subject to many different opinions and separate perspectives. For her to gain the most accurate understanding of her strengths and weaknesses, she needed to turn to herself.

Do you remember the last time you took a test? If you studied, you probably breezed through it confidently. If you didn't study, you were most likely insecure, nervous, and forced to guess your way through the most difficult questions. The results of neglecting studies no doubt showed up on your report card. Life is often like a report card; it tells us exactly how we're doing when we take the time to read it. If you're honest, you can look at your own life and grade yourself with great accuracy.

As you read this chapter, think about the quality or condition of your individuality. Consider how you think and speak. What are your thought patterns, communication trends, and vocabulary choices? Be open to thought-provoking questions that will help you hunt down your weaknesses and gather your strengths. Ask yourself what your life is saying about you.

In any journey of self-discovery, one must commit to reporting the truth no matter how incriminating it appears to be. This is the only way to achieve an honest evaluation of how you are doing. Looking at yourself through a magnifying glass will give you the sobering details you need to understand your communication health and determine the soil from which your words grow.

In an interview, you are most vulnerable when you don't know your subject. Every interview is an "inner-view" of you, which is why you must be the authority on yourself.

THE 80/20 PRINCIPLE

The 80/20 principle provides a framework for developing a better understanding of yourself. Essentially, this principle says that each of us are 80% strengths and 20% weaknesses. No matter how successful and confident we appear, no one is 100% perfect.

The language of 80/20 is the ebb and flow of your strengths and weaknesses. It is a skillful dance that can only be mastered through determination, discipline, and a positive attitude. Let's give them the attention they deserve by purposely putting them in their place!

In the activity at the end of this chapter, you'll be challenged to create your own 80/20 lists. To determine your personal 80/20, you will need to identify, define, and "prove" words that describe you. When you are doing this, you must list the facts and trust your findings.

When I first did this exercise, I wrote down as many strengths as I could think of. Focusing first on my top five, I defined each one to make sure my understanding of the word was accurate. Then, I identified the ways in which I applied these strengths to my daily life.

I wrote down:

1. **Loyal. (Giving or showing firm and constant support or allegiance to a person or institution.)** I was always there for those that needed me.

2. **Gentle. (Mild in temperament or behavior. Kind or tender.)** I was sensitive to the needs of others and served as a calming influence in times of crisis.

3. **Content. (Being in a state of peaceful happiness. Satisfied with a certain level of achievement.)** I was content with people's flaws and even my own, but I also knew I didn't need more flaws.

4. **Determined. (Having made a firm decision and a resolve not to change it.)** My determination helped me overcome many obstacles and has helped encourage others to do the same.

5. **Compassionate. (Feeling or showing sympathy and concern for others.)** I provide others with comfort and calming encouragement all the time.

As I studied these five particular strengths, it was as if a lightbulb went on. I was truly equipped to make a positive difference in any circumstance. These characteristics were part of the very fiber of my being. If I didn't use them, that would be my choice, but it would be going against who I really was.

Here is my complete list:

80%	20%
Positive	Stubborn
Motivated	Judgmental
Determined	Short-tempered
Compassionate	Unforgiving
Loyal	Lazy
Content	
Spirit-filled	
Gentle	
Honest	

When you start to compile your own list, pay close attention to the meaning of the words that you've selected. If you don't know undoubtedly that you own that characteristic, you can't claim it!

For example, you may believe that you are positively equipped with resourcefulness. However, when you look it up in the dictionary, you can't relate to the definition. When you search for evidence of such a trait, you can't find any examples in your life to prove it. In this case, you simply need to dig a little deeper to find the right word to describe yourself.

Think of discovering your 80/20 like reading a treasure map for the first time. You may be eager to get to the treasure, but you must first uncover each clue and determine its meaning.

DON'T LET YOUR 20% DEFINE YOU

After they've created their personal 80/20, people will sometimes be discouraged by their weaknesses. They say to me, "I can't help it. This is just the way I am." I get it, it is easy to become limited by our 20%. Just because this is the way you act, doesn't mean this is the way you *should act*. You may be wired a certain way, but with some investment in yourself you can control the way you act and react.

You are taking steps toward the Power Seat as you gain momentum, armed with the knowledge of who you are. Knowledge is power. With this introspective mindset, you will be fully trained with resourceful strengths. You will also be able to recognize and head off the 20% before it becomes a wrecking ball of destruction that destroys relationships, opportunities, and communication success.

You are bursting with undeveloped potential, but you can't rely upon, justify, or protect your weaknesses while claiming to be loyal to your strengths. That would be like dancing with the hero and the villain at the same time. Remember, your 20% and your 80% are equally important. They both have the power to shape the course of your life.

It is painful to realize that you may be your own worst enemy, holding onto your 20% like it was all you had to work with. Do not let that 20% define you. Your 20% can be destructive, prideful, and undisciplined—think of it as a spoiled and immature child. Sometimes kids (even adults) can act like bullies because they're afraid of being bullied themselves. Bullies intimidate and create fear to get their way. This is exactly how your inner enemy works.

When my 20% was in control, fear, intimidation, and justification were its goal. If you are sheltering your 20%, it's understandable. Many of us fear exposing our vulnerable, humble, and authentic self. If we silence our enemy, we are left without a "tough guy" in our corner. Your 20% has nothing good planned for you. It will hide behind your excuses as long as you provide them. Stop feeding the negative part of yourself and start nourishing the positive part. Once you do this, the bully within becomes diminutive, quiet, ineffective, and less significant.

When you're 20% list is complete, you will be ready to make a bold statement. One that calls out your villain and sets the stage for new leadership. Calling out your villains will set the stage for new leadership. Your 20% is only a small part of you; it's not the most important part of you, so don't give it more power than it deserves. We all have good and bad in us. It's what we choose to listen to that makes the difference.

COMMUNICATING FROM A PLACE OF STRENGTH

Once you identify the strengths that comprise 80%, you can then work on using your characteristics to become a more effective communicator. Making an effort to communicate from a place of strength will improve your personal and professional relationships in addition to helping you ace your next interview.

We can infuse hope or draw blood with the words we say. If you don't believe me, think about the best book you've ever read. A skilled author knows how to choose words that evoke emotions, tell a story, and keep the reader captivated. Every avid reader I know has experienced times where they've wanted to leave the laundry undone, order takeout from their favorite Chinese restaurant, and curl up with a great book so they can find out what happens next. Whether the story ultimately leaves them jumping for joy or crying tears of sorrow, that's proof that words have power.

Getting to the Power Seat is about knowledge and responsibility. We have a responsibility to make wise use of the knowledge we've gained about our personal strengths and weaknesses. Communicating with impact and intent must start with the resolve that failure is not an option. We can all be selfless, honest, resourceful, and powerful interviewees with the right insight. Therefore, we must go all out to know, understand, accept, and trust who we are in order to reflect ourselves accurately.

LISTEN WITH YOUR STRENGTHS

To sit in the Power Seat as an effective communicator, you must learn to listen with your strengths. How we hear what the other party is saying determines how we think about our response. If we aren't listening effectively, we can't formulate a response that delivers an honest message.

Here are seven examples of listening with your strengths, based on a sample set of my own strengths:

1. *Generous:* A Power Seat communicator provides an open floor for conversation. Be willing to put yourself second when necessary to advance the dialogue.

2. *Objective:* Strive to hear without prejudice. An open mind is essential for clear communication.

3. *Positive:* Negativity has no place in the Power Seat. When you allow hope and possibility to develop, you'll be thrilled with the results!

4. *Honest:* Setting the stage for genuine thought ensures a successful conversation. Tell the truth, even when it's painful.

5. *Attentive:* A successful communicator makes an effort to be both physically and mentally present. Make sure to catch the relevant details and important information. If you need to, carry a small notepad to jot down your thoughts.

6. *Patient:* Assume the Power Seat by giving the speaker a calming environment and laying the groundwork for detailed thought to occur.

7. *Humble:* In today's society, being humble is often thought of as a weakness. However, this couldn't be further from the truth. A strong communicator is humble enough to accept and learn from others.

Here are seven examples of listening with your weakness, based on my own sample profile:

1. *Selfish:* You are being selfish if you find yourself wanting the conversation to be about you. A conversation involves give and take. Your goal should be to learn about the other party.

2. *Impatient:* Patience is a virtue when you're preparing to take the Power Seat. Successful communicators don't cut others off as they are rushing to get to the next subject.

3. *Skeptical:* Having strongly held convictions is an admirable character trait, but so is open mindedness. Make an effort to listen to another perspective, even if you're 100% convinced that your mind is already made up.

4. *Negative:* Limiting the potential and direction of a conversation shows your weakness as a communicator. Wanting to stay on topic is fine, but you must be open to minor detours that can enhance the overall quality of the discussion.

5. *Inattentive:* When you're asked to listen, you must be attentive to the speaker's key points. Being unable to give back to the conversation keeps you from claiming your position in the Power Seat.

6. *Nervous:* When you're nervous, you're unable to retain important and relevant facts. Don't let the jitters get the best of you!

7. *Prideful:* Being prideful makes it hard to admit when you've made a mistake or to honestly evaluate another point of view.

THINK THROUGH YOUR STRENGTHS

We think in the same way as we listen. Consequently, the tone in which we think is set by how we listen. If you are listening selfishly, you can't be thinking generously.

You must expect, imagine, and anticipate your thoughts. If you don't, your thoughts morph into weakness. Thinking through your strengths is a call to become more proactive and powerful.

There are three important reasons why you must learn to think through your strengths before assuming the Power Seat in your interview:

1. When you allow yourself time to think, you not only project your targeted strengths, but you slow down the conversation. This makes for the perfect climate to have a meaningful and memorable dialogue.

2. Thinking through your strengths will keep your mind busy. This means you will have no time to be nervous.

3. If you fail to think through your strengths, you are likely to manifest traces of weakness. Letting negativity, impatience, pride, or any of your 20% qualities creep into the conversation effectively sabotages your chance for success.

SPEAK FROM YOUR STRENGTHS

Your words define you. They are the most valuable tool you will ever have, so use them wisely.

Here are some examples of speaking from strengths, based on my own sample strengths:

1. *Generous:* "Please take as much time as you need to discuss my qualifications. I am happy to provide any additional information that might be helpful."

2. *Objective:* "I can work with others that do not share my same opinions."

3. *Positive:* "My last job was great in so many ways. I appreciated all that I learned and look forward to the same opportunities wherever I am hired."

4. *Honest:* "I have many strengths I am eager to offer. Although organization is not one of them at the moment, it is never too late to work on it."

5. *Attentive:* "It is clear you care deeply for the mission of this company. I would be honored to help you achieve your goals."

6. *Patient:* "If you need clarification, I would be happy to go over it again."

7. *Humble:* "Even though I know I am qualified for this position, I believe I still have much that I can learn from the other professionals at your company."

Here are some examples of speaking from weakness, based on my own sample weaknesses:

1. *Selfish:* "If I am hired, when will I get my first raise?"

2. *Impatient:* "I don't need to know all the details until I have the job."

3. *Skeptical:* "Are you sure this is the correct list of tasks in the job description? It seems wrong."

4. *Negative:* "I was unhappy at my last job because my coworkers weren't respectful of my contributions, and my manager asked for duties that were above and beyond my stated job description."

5. *Inattentive:* "Sorry, I didn't catch that. Could you repeat that last statement?"

6. *Nervous:* "I forgot what I was saying."

7. *Prideful:* "I graduated at the top of my class and have won multiple awards for my performance. I am sure you will not find another applicant as qualified as I am."

POINTS TO REMEMBER

- The 80/20 principle reflects the simple truth that none of us are perfect. Our personalities are comprised of 80% strengths and 20% weaknesses. Successful people are simply those who have learned to make full use of their 80% while minimizing the damaging effects of their 20%.

- Your personality is always a work in progress. Even if you've been ruled by your 20% before, there's still opportunity for growth and change. Anyone who tells you that making a positive change is hopeless simply needs more hope!

- To claim the Power Seat, strive to communicate from a place of strength. Your words are what define you, so choose them carefully. Listen, think, and speak with your 80%. When this becomes a habit, there's no limit to what you can accomplish.

Activity: Uncovering Your 80/20

*"Success is achieved by developing our strengths,
not by eliminating our weaknesses." – Marilyn vos Savant*

For this activity the following forms will provide you an opportunity to identify, define, and prove your own strengths and weaknesses. If you would like to download the forms as well, please visit thepowerseat.com. Remember, the 80% represents all the positive character trait strengths you have, while the 20% represents your personal weaknesses.

Begin the 80% side with a collection of your personal strengths. Once you have a good list underway, begin your 20% column by listing your weaknesses. Make sure to write in pencil so you can make adjustments later if needed.

While studying yourself, you will likely change your mind about which words best describe your personality. As you list your qualities, use a dictionary or thesaurus to check your understanding of the meaning of each word. To begin the process of change, you must make sure your understanding of the definitions is accurate. Definitions become watered down over time. In some instances, they change in our understanding of them altogether.

Your list should reflect an honest assessment and not merely parrot the observations of others. It can be tempting to want to take ownership of what your mother, father, spouse, or friend has told you about yourself. Avoid that impulse. It's important that these qualities are truthfully stated and proven in your life, both through your actions and through your words. Turn to actual events or circumstances in your life and relationships to verify where you see either a strength or a weakness show up.

Once these columns are full, you can figure out which side is dominating your actions, reactions, functions, and dysfunctions. We often see after this exercise that we are not tapping into the 80%, and the 20% has taken over. The proof always lies in the facts. How you respond to people, circumstances, stress, and change are all derived from a strength or weakness.

Any time we trust our weaknesses to do the talking, they will. If you are not in the moment with your strength, you are in the moment with your weakness. Rest assured, it will be evident through your circumstance. You can't have both strength and weakness in the same moment.

80% — Strengths		
Identify Strength	Define (Definition)	Prove (How you know this is your strength)
Strategic	Relating to the identification of long-term or overall aims and interests and the means of achieving them.	I organize each day and plan how to achieve my goals. I enjoy solving problems and staying organized.

20% — Weaknesses		
Identify Trait	Define	Prove
Comparing	Estimate, measure, or note the similarity or dissimilarity between.	Measure my value against the accomplishments of others.

Activity: The Strength Box

*"Right now my life is one learning experience after another.
By the end of the week I should be a genius." – Jeanette Osias*

The strength box provides a different way to help you identify your abilities. Be completely honest when recording your answers. It's important to keep in mind that none of us fit perfectly into a box. We are all unique individuals. This is only an example to get you thinking about yourself from different angles.

Once you are done studying the chart, choose what color you are most like. Hopefully, you will find many of the same traits that you listed in your 80% column. If you don't, go back to your original 80/20 chart and consider how honestly you completed the exercise.

Put a number between 0-3 behind every adjective. Once you have done this, tally up your numbers. Based on your total, you can see what color column you are most like. When you've identified with a color column, cross-reference it with your 80/20 list. See if you can find some unique parallels or consistencies that solidify your strengths, abilities, talents, and unique character traits.

3 = very much like me	1 = somewhat like me
2 = quite a bit like me	0 = not like me

Blue	Red	Green	Yellow
Altruistic / Nurturing	Assertive / Directing	Analytical / Realistic	Flexible / Cohering
trusting	self-confident	cautious	flexible
optimistic	enterprising	practical	open to change
loyal	ambitious	economical	socializer
idealistic	organizer	reserved	experimenter
helpful	persuasive	methodical	curious
modest	forceful	analytical	adaptable
devoted	quick-to-act	principled	tolerant
caring	imaginative	orderly	open to compromise
supportive	competitive	fair	looks for options
accepting	risk-taker	persevering	socially sensitive
total:	total:	total:	total:

This graph is based on Personal Assessment Service, Inc.

Remember that your distinctive strengths are what will set you apart from others. It's incredible to think how so many people desperately try to be different from their true selves through imitation. The way to be unique is by being yourself! None of us stand out by imitation.

Imitation is limitation in most cases. As we learn to trust our strengths and deny our weaknesses, we become believable in our own eyes. The power of 80/20 is not hard to learn. If you don't use it, however, you will lose it!

Activity: Practice Makes Perfect

"Take advantage of every opportunity to practice your communication skills so that when occasions arise, you will have the gift, style, sharpness, clarity, and emotions to penetrate and affect other people." – Jim Rohn

I bet it's safe to say that whatever you are currently doing successfully is the result of extensive practice. Whether it be a hobby, project, vacation, diet, or climbing to the top of Mount Everest, your mind granted you the permission to accomplish it, and your practice helped you hone the necessary skills.

In *Outliers*, Malcolm Gladwell states that it takes 10,000 hours of practice to become an expert in anything. "Practice isn't the thing you do once you're good," he writes. "It's the thing you do that makes you good."

This means you can expect that making meaningful changes to your communication style isn't going to happen overnight. You've taken the first steps in a journey toward self-improvement, but you're not going to reach your final goal in the next day or two.

In this activity, I want you to make an effort to be an active and attentive listener for the next three days. List your own strengths and weaknesses, going back to your personal 80/20 list. When you're finished, challenge yourself to identify examples of times when you've listened from a place of strength as well as moments in which you let your weaknesses get the better of you.

Listening from Strength

1._____

2._____

3._____

4._____

5._____

6._____

7._____

8._____

9._____

10._____

Now, consider the various conversations you've had with friends, family, and professional associates. Write down the times in which you listened from your weaknesses.

Listening from Weakness

1. _____

2. _____

3. _____

4. _____

5. _____

6. _____

7. _____

8. _____

9. _____

10. _____

Anytime you are speaking from a strength you are tapping into a powerful resource. Try to recall conversations where you spoke through your identified strengths.

Speaking from Strength

1. _____

2. _____

3. _____

4. _____

5. _____

6. _____

7. _____

8. _____

9. _____

10. _____

THE POWER OF 80/20

Typically, when we speak from our 20% we don't leave the conversation feeling so great. Be as honest as possible and describe where, when, why, and to whom you spoke from your weakness. You may see a pattern in your answers. If so, try to figure out the reason for it.

Speaking from Weakness

1. _____

2. _____

3. _____

4. _____

5. _____

6. _____

7. _____

8. _____

9. _____

10. _____

Chapter 3:
Set Your Mind in the
Right Place for Success

"Nothing is at last sacred but the integrity of our own mind."
– Ralph Waldo Emerson

Not long ago, I met a man named Augie Nieto. Augie is the founder and retired CEO of Life Fitness, a company that specializes in the production and distribution of fitness equipment. He was diagnosed with Amyotrophic Lateral Sclerosis, or ALS, in 2005 at only 47 years old.

Augie's diagnosis has not extinguished his determination to be exceptional, but it has forced him to channel his strengths in a different way. He is the founder of Augie's Quest, a nonprofit organization that raises money to find a cure for ALS. Augie's Quest has raised over $45 million since 2006 to benefit ALS TDI, the world's largest ALS-dedicated drug development organization. These funds have helped launch clinical trials and fund the development of medications with the potential to save the lives of millions of people.

For Augie, losing his means to communicate has always been out of the question. He is unable to speak, but he uses special machines to translate his thoughts onto a screen. He has published two books that were written with his toes, bringing his unique message of hope and positivity to people all around the world.

It's obvious that Augie's mind is set for success, regardless of the obstacles he must endure. He is willing to let go of past disappointments to prepare for a brighter future. Let him inspire you to look at challenges as opportunities in disguise.

THE SUPPORT OF YOUR MIND

Have you ever tried to accomplish something thoughtlessly, without fully engaging your mind to understand the task? Perhaps you set a New Year's resolution to lose 10 pounds without actually planning how you were going to accomplish this goal. Since you didn't have a plan in your mind, you were unable to wake up early to go the gym, and you failed to resist the temptation of stopping at the bakery each day for a double chocolate fudge cupcake. Eventually, you gave up your dream of rocking those new skinny jeans. What you may not have realized is that your failure was the result of a mindless effort. In order to succeed in any goal, you must fully enlist your mind to support the cause.

Your mind sets the bar for the level of belief and trust you put in your abilities. You're reading this book, which means right now is the best time to step up and manage your mind. Do not be discouraged if you've been off the job for a while or you're embarking on a new career path. It is never too late to change the way you manage your mind.

Your insecurities live only in your mind. Your conscious mind is simply a product of what you have taught it and how you have trained it. Start by going over your facts. It is impossible to be secure and certain without the truth.

Here are some facts about me:

- I am a simple girl.

- I live a simple life.

- I am not a scholar.

These facts don't deter me from being a confident interview coach. I'm an expert in interviewing because of my life experiences and my endless studies in that area. I have taught myself to recognize and utilize my strengths. I actively work to avoid letting my weaknesses take control of my destiny. What about you?

The insecurities we battle are a result of being unfamiliar with the facts of who we are. Imagine you had a job where you had to sell a product you didn't understand. What if you were charged with selling expensive wine even though you did not drink alcohol? You would have no choice but to fake your sales pitch every time. You would likely become bored and discouraged by your lack of success as a salesperson. Ultimately, you'd look for another place to work that was more in line with your interests and abilities.

What if one day you stumbled upon something unexpected about the product? Perhaps your perceived dislike of wine was simply because you had only tried white wine. Then, once you took the time to sip a glass of your employer's red wine, you discovered that those blueberry and blackberry notes were what you'd been searching for your entire life. With this new knowledge, I bet you'd become more confident, enthusiastic, and invested in your role as a wine salesperson.

In an interview, the state of your mind will be what determines your success. Set your mind, and the rest will follow. I promise there is no challenge your mind can't overcome.

I once had a client who was blessed with a beautiful voice. Sadly, every time she auditioned, her voice cracked. Eventually, she stopped singing because she convinced herself that she was unable to stop her voice from being compromised when under stress. By ending her dream, she unknowingly became the victim of failing to understand and train her own mind to lead her to success.

In my 25 years of working with women, I've found their most common complaint is that they feel insecure about who they really are. Living with the uncertainty of your abilities is bound to stop you from believing in them. This emanates from not knowing enough about who you really are, not training your mind to accept you for who you really are, and allowing these issues to prevent you from capitalizing on who you really are.

When I share this with my clients, I compare it to walking in super high heels. It's awkward at first. You feel uncoordinated and clumsy while trying to look confident and stable. However, if you convince your mind that you're going to walk like a runway model, one foot in front of the other, heel, toe, heel, toe, twisting on the ball of your foot, with a light landing and an attitude, you will. It's all about controlling and convincing your mind!

When we change the inner attitudes of our minds, we change the outer aspects of our lives. Manage your thoughts with responsible leadership that is educated, intentional, and wise. Remember, your thoughts show up in your words and your words define you.

THE BUILDING BLOCKS OF SUCCESS

Let's put this concept to work by exploring some ways to get you and your mind reacquainted. Some of these practices will seem easier than others. Consider putting a star next to those that seem most challenging so you can refer back to them at a later date. Those exercises will give you the greatest potential for growth! Here are 10 challenges just for your mind.

1. Track the patterns of your mind.

Years ago, I worked with a young lady who was pursuing a career in politics. She spent all her time studying the mannerisms, speaking patterns, and philosophies of the various politicians she admired. When it came time to express her individuality, she was lost. She had spent all her time imitating other politicians and had no idea what unique perspective she could bring to the table.

To win over supporters, she needed to study her mind. Who wants to vote for a politician who doesn't have a clear view of who she is and what she wants to accomplish?

It is a good idea to keep a journal that lets you investigate the habits your mind is keeping. We can go a lifetime and overlook the bad habits we have allowed our minds to adopt. It takes a conscious effort to realize the counterproductive behaviors of your mind.

If you hate to write, don't worry. Your journal doesn't need to be worthy of a Pulitzer Prize. Spelling and grammar errors are okay, since this is simply a tool for self-reflection. If you're more of a visual learner, you can even organize your thoughts as a list, outline, or collection of doodles! Since your journal is for your own personal use, it doesn't matter what it looks like to others.

Consider these questions as you journal:

- Does your mind wander? If so, how often, and for how long?

- Is your mind undisciplined? When?

- Do you trust where it goes? Do you intentionally lead it astray?

- Is your mind set in its ways, unwilling to change? In what specific areas?

Remember that your greatest answer to any question lies within you. Your mind is desperate to be led. You need to direct it toward responsible patterns that deliver results of certainty.

2. Visualize your mind.

My mind is a small lake that reflects like glass. Around the perimeter of my mind is long, green, whimsical grass that blows sideways. It is deep with knowledge, but has a shallow side that is not as attractive.

How does your mind look to you? Is it a river, running rapid, or a green pasture with vibrant wild flowers? If you have never tried to imagine such a thing before, you are missing out. Visualizing your mind brings it to a new level of awareness. Your mind is capable of great things, so don't be afraid to bring it to life in your imagination!

Even if you're not normally a crafty person, I have a DIY project I'd like to you try. Select a large sheet of poster board in your favorite color. Create a collage from magazine clippings, postcards, photographs, and other images to represent how you visualize your mind. If desired, use a marker or pencil to add words, phrases, or quotes that reflect your visualization. When you're finished, hang your artwork in an area where you'll see it every morning. This will provide you with a constant reminder of your mind's power.

As we become more familiar with our minds, we become more accountable to our thoughts. When your mind becomes relatable, trusting it and respecting it become much easier.

3. Start a dialogue with your mind.

Dialogue refers to a conversation or an exchange. Your mind will respond to your call if you are honest and brave. Start by acknowledging the positive areas of your mind that please you. Offer up some sincere compliments coupled with a hearty pep talk concerning your future goals.

Try saying these words:

- "I am grateful for your knowledge."

- "I'm sorry for neglecting you."

- "I want to encourage you to stay sharp, discerning, and eager to learn new ways."

- "I have goals and plans for us to make a positive difference and accomplish great things!"

Set a new tone for strong leadership and direction by focusing on your areas of weakness and working to eliminate bad habits. Your weaknesses may have moved in and become very comfortable living in your mind. Expect some rebellious behavior. Old habits take time to kill off.

4. Test your mind.

We have all taken plenty of tests in our lives. They are not always fun, but they are helpful in revealing how much we really know.

Since you are studying yourself, finding ways to test your mind on the language of your 80/20 is important. Understanding how much you know about who you really are will help you be the best person possible. The more you know yourself, the more you can rely on what you know to guide you through the challenges you'll encounter on a daily basis.

Start by asking your mind to recite your strengths and weaknesses. Work from the top of the list down, and then switch directions until you have it memorized. Try writing out scenarios that might happen in your personal life and testing your mind on how you would respond.

Try challenging yourself to a mock interview of your own. This provides an opportunity for you to test your mind on its reliability with the tools you have already gathered from the previous chapters. Here are some questions to use for this exercise:

- "What are three positive things others would say about you?"
- "What is your biggest achievement in life so far?"
- "How would you describe your leadership style?"
- "How do you handle conflict with others?"
- "When faced with a difficult challenge, what do you do to solve the problem?"
- "Do you prefer to work alone or as part of a team?"
- "What are your goals?"

- "What are your weaknesses?"

- "What can you offer our company if you're selected for this opportunity?"

- "Why are you interested in this opportunity?"

5. Exercise your mind.

You can train your mind in the same way you train your body. Turn off the TV, get up from the couch, and make a conscious effort to strengthen your mind. Every day is an opportunity for your mind to shine.

Try learning a new language or reading short stories and reciting as many facts as possible about what you read. Play Sudoku, tackle crossword puzzles, or go to a website like lumosity.com to exercise your mind in new and challenging ways. Create a baseline so you can track your progress over time. Consider how powerful you'll be by cultivating the presence of concentration to get that brain fit and strong!

You can build mental muscle as you go about your daily routine by challenging yourself to remember the names of all the people you meet. As your mind gets stronger, try committing to memory specific facts about these men and women. Were they energetic, calm, focused, or distracted? Did they ramble or get right to the point? Did they smile at all? What was unique about their style of conversation? You would be surprised how many facts you can gather, even from a short exchange while you're picking up your morning coffee.

If you're notoriously absent-minded, you may have to work harder at this exercise. Forgetting names is often an indicator that you are not fully invested in the moment with your mind. Fortunately, you'll find that your memory grows stronger each day as you actively work at overcoming your forgetful tendencies.

6. Prepare your mind to learn.

I worked with a client for weeks before we both realized we were getting nowhere. Ruth was frustrated and unable to focus. After discussing her difficulties at length, I discovered she was working two jobs, in a bad relationship, and not taking care of herself. She was struggling to benefit from our sessions because she was mentally exhausted. Ruth was running at a fast pace with no time to listen or learn.

You can't expect to master new skills when your environment doesn't support learning. It may be a battle to prepare an acceptable learning environment for your mind, but you must have faith in your ability to persevere. If you're in Ruth's situation, commit to making yourself a priority by forgoing an hour or two of television each week, enlisting your spouse or children to help with the housework, or getting up a bit earlier so you have some time for quiet reflection each morning. It might feel awkward at first, but we have to plan ahead for the knowledge we need to be wise and confident individuals.

If you are not preparing your mind, your mind will leave you unprepared. Start by thinking out of the ordinary. Consider the following brain-boosting activities:

- Sign up for educational seminars about a topic of professional or personal interest. You can often find seminars at your local community college.

- Listen to random speakers covering topics you've always wanted to know more about. TED talks are particularly fascinating, covering everything from the power of introverts to how gaming can make the world a better place.

- Give a presentation on a special interest you want others to learn more about.

- Compile a list of what you will need to grow in knowledge, focus, and perspective. Post this list someplace where you can refer to it daily to help keep you motivated.

- Set time aside with family and ask for feedback on where they think you can improve. Accept their input with a grateful heart, even if some of their advice is a blow to your ego.

7. Give your mind variety.

Never trying anything new can get old fast. Our minds get bored and need a change of pace. Take your mind exploring. Find a museum, mountain, lake, ocean, or park to encourage new energy and true motivation. If you are always buried in some form of social media, get out from under it and give your mind a refreshing environment to learn in. Try writing a letter or poem. Try a yoga class, or train to run your first 5K.

You can also find the cure for boredom in your 80/20 facts list. Studying your strengths is interesting, but understanding your weaknesses and visualizing how they will limit you and your relationships is even better.

The challenge to stay fresh in your mind will not always be easy. We are creatures of habit, so you must stay proactive!

8. Pay attention to your diet.

My grandma is 95 years old. She has been eating a balanced diet for as long as I can remember. She splurges occasionally but generally takes her diet very seriously. She will testify that although there are certain things we can't control in our lives, your diet is something you can easily change to further your goals.

When you fuel your mind with nutritious foods, you will see the results in how you think. Blackberries, apples, chocolate, cinnamon, spinach, extra virgin olive oil, salmon, curry, and Concord grape juice are just a few of the foods that have been proven to energize, sharpen, and support overall health. A personal favorite for me, although it is an acquired taste, is turmeric root. I usually get it in powder form and put it in smoothies and over rice. It's known for healing your mind. When mixed with royal jelly, it also works as a rejuvenating face mask!

It takes discipline to properly nourish your mind. However, knowing that you are what you eat might be your best motivation.

9. Rest your mind.

I have a client who lives in New York City. She told me she was playing a game with friends one night where the challenge was to describe your current environment in one word. She wrote "overstimulation" and went on to tell me the constant feeling of being overstimulated was taking a toll on her overall well-being. She struggled to find quiet moments during her day. For the longest time, she complained about the concert pianist practicing above her at night until a friend heard it and loved how relaxing it was. My client decided to turn a negative into a positive and use the piano music to calm her mind. Most of us will struggle to find the "perfect" environment we need to calm down and rest. Like my client, sometimes we just need to change our attitude about our environment. Try and find peace in your circumstances by searching for the positive in it.

We have endless opportunities to make the most of ourselves and our communication, but we often miss them when we are too tired. You need support, strength, encouragement, and rest to be your best self. I have many clients who practice yoga. I have other clients who pray and dedicate 20 minutes a day to being completely alone with God. Your method of resting is up to you, as long as it helps you recharge and prepare to face the day ahead.

10. Lead your mind.

Imagine that you are the only adult chaperone on a bus with 10 middle school students. You are deep in the mountains when the bus suddenly crashes. A storm has come in, and the roads have closed. No one has a working cell phone. It is getting dark. The kids are physically unharmed, but they are scared, crying, hungry, and cold. The driver needs medical attention. No one knows you have crashed. You are the obvious choice as the leader of the group. What would you do first to take control of the situation?

Some of us are natural leaders, while others have to work harder at knowing when to take control. The great part about unexpected leadership opportunities is that they let reluctant leaders realize their untapped inner potential.

In my community, there are some really great leaders. I have noticed that each one of them believes deeply in the cause they lead. You must **believe** in yourself in order to lead your mind. You, my friend, are the cause. Don't think for one moment you are not equipped to lead your mind. If you aren't, no one is!

You will find the motivation, courage, and passion to step up as a leader when you become committed to who you know you can be. Your mind is worth the investment, but you have to believe in order to achieve. It's tempting to want to make excuses or discredit your abilities, but you are prepared. Get excited and believe in the knowledge you are getting through studying yourself.

POINTS TO REMEMBER

- The state of your mind is what determines your success. With the right attitude, there's no limit to what you can accomplish.

- Training your mind to be successful requires small adjustments to your daily routine. Strive to learn something new every day, strengthen your mental muscles, eat well, and get the rest you need to recharge your mind.

- Even if you don't think of yourself as a writer, consider keeping a journal to track and evaluate the patterns of your mind. This will help you better understand who you are as a person and what steps must be taken to reach your goals.

_____

_____

_____

_____

_____

_____

_____

Activity: Putting the 10 Challenges into Action

"The mind is like a parachute,
it doesn't work unless it's open." – Unknown

My mind has lived with me for 47 years. It has many moods and tends to be lazy. I know that little sleep, poor diet, and extreme stress can trigger episodes of amnesia. With stubborn opposition, my mind avoids change at every turn. Fortunately, I know my mind wants to please me. The more I provide positive reinforcement and call upon it to perform, the more it delivers.

Being able to describe my mind took patience and dedication. For this activity, I want you to become more familiar with your mind by taking the 10 challenges from this chapter and putting them into motion! Assign a challenge to each day for the next 10 days. You can follow them in order or choose your own path.

Keep a journal where you reflect on your mind's reactions. Write a concluding entry at the end of the 10 days on how you've grown into a powerful individual. (If you feel as though one challenge is significantly more difficult than the others, remember that it's OK to go back and try again. Self-improvement is an ongoing process. Recognizing areas where you need a little extra help is the sign of someone ready to assume the Power Seat.)

1. Track the patterns of your mind.

2. Visualize your mind.

3. Start a dialogue with your mind.

4. Test your mind.

5. Exercise your mind.

6. Prepare your mind to learn.

7. Give your mind variety.

8. Pay attention to your diet.

9. Rest your mind.

10. Lead your mind.

Activity: Question Yourself

"Ignorance is a temporary affliction,
remedied only by asking the right questions." – Colin Wright

With each chapter, you are getting closer to understanding the Power Seat way. You must know when you are prepared as yourself; you will never be unprepared being yourself. This concept is fundamental and invaluable.

Would you want to know in advance what questions were going to be asked of you in an interview? I bet you said yes! Who wouldn't want to know? It's a curiosity that is hard to ignore. After all, if we knew in advance, we could rehearse for the answers, right? I touched on this earlier. We can only guess what questions will be asked. We will never know for sure.

Today, you can go online and find hundreds of potential questions pertaining to interview preparation. Unfortunately, they are the wrong kind of questions. They prepare us to be unprepared.

The surest approach is to prepare in the certainty of your strengths, weaknesses, beliefs, and capabilities. We can study and rehearse generic questions all day long. However, in doing so, we run the risk of having an ordinary, average, and powerless interview.

The following questions are going to help you prepare for your next interview. Remember, you are studying yourself. Answer the questions without excuses. Be brave, specific, and honest. You are now embarking upon the facts of what make you unique, set apart, and a priceless candidate for any job!

- Do you enjoy yourself?

- Does anyone you respect also respect you?

- Are you harder on yourself or others?

- Do you turn toward culture to define yourself?

- How do you feel about people seeing your flaws?

- What do you spend your time doing when you are alone?

- How often are you smiling?

- How often do you say sorry?

- Are you a giver or a taker?

- Do you brag often in conversations?

- Are you a good friend? If so, why?

- If you had to write your own obituary, what would it say?

- How do you respond to criticism?

- Do you always think you are right?

- Do you trust easily?

- Do you ever ask for forgiveness?

- Would you be able to write an instructional manual about yourself?

- Do you think before you speak or speak without thinking?

- How often do you thank others for their contributions?

- Do you cry? If so, how often? Why?

- Do you wait for others to volunteer first? Why?

- How many people are you currently fighting with?

- Are you relieved when others are worse off than you? Why?

- Are you always the victim of something? Why?

- Do you always have a bigger and better story than the one you heard? Why?

- When others are gossiping, do you opt out or join in?

- Are you out of shape and unhealthy? Why?

- Are most of the people you have friendships with popular?

- How much time do you spend talking about other people's lives? Why?

- Do you compare yourself with others to feel better or worse? Why?

- Are you attracted to drama in your life? Why?

- Are you cynical? Why?

- Why wouldn't someone want to hire you?

- Do you suck the energy out of others?

- Does the truth threaten you?

- How many times do you look at yourself in the mirror a day?

- Would you rather give a compliment or get one?

- What is your daily purpose?

- Do you look for answers or do you settle for problems?

- Are you afraid to know yourself?

- Are you focused on feelings or facts?

- Do you stand out in a crowd?

- Do you compromise in order to be liked?

- Do you pretend to be friendly and when the person leaves devalue them? If so, why?

- Do you complain in your daily conversations?

- Would you be happy if you saw yourself coming into a room?

- What is your reputation within your family?

- What is your reputation in your community?

- What is your reputation among your friends?

Hopefully, your 80% is alive and active in your answers. But, perhaps there were times you recognized your 20% lurking. These are challenging questions, and certainly they can make us uncomfortable.

The purpose is not to beat yourself up, but rather to confront your own reality.

As an interviewee, you must not be concerned with what the listener is thinking, but rather the intent, motive, and conviction of what you are saying. The wrong motive can happen without us even thinking about it. This is why we go through the journey and the practice of asking the hard questions of ourselves before the interview takes place.

With the Power Seat approach, you can feel confident that when the time comes you will know the good, bad, and ugly of all your motives so you can intentionally select the right ones.

Chapter 4:
Settle Your Past

"If you are carrying strong feelings about something that happened in your past, they may hinder your ability to live in the present." – Les Brown

The challenge to choose between yesterday and tomorrow is scary, but there are three things you must remember:

- People who live in the past live with regret.

- People who live in the future live with anxiety.

- People who live in the moment live in peace.

The way you feel about your past, present, and future has more to do with how you handle your interview than you might know. I have yet to meet a highly successful communicator who lives with an unsettled past. There isn't room for success and failure in the same intentional thought.

In some ways, settling the past is like cleaning out our closets and having to get rid of the clothes that represent where we have been. It is a tedious job that only gets done after a million excuses. We want to avoid that dreadful and all too permanent farewell.

When the job is done, however, all those clothes we couldn't bear to part with are soon forgotten. We discover that we didn't really need the evening gown from 1987 or the swimsuit that hasn't fit in six years. We are funny that way—holding on simply because we are afraid to let go. We must remember that what we don't need, we shouldn't have.

I was laughing with a friend the other day whose problem literally involved cleaning the closet. She would do just about anything to avoid doing laundry. However, her dislike for laundry caught up with her when the hose to her washing machine broke. Because my friend avoided the laundry room, the broken hose went undetected until an even bigger problem was discovered…mold!

Bypassing the laundry room to avoid an unpleasant household chore is similar to what we do with our past. The laundry will not take care of itself and neither will your past. However, with the right perspective and a new attitude, the laundry room might become your favorite room in the house!

The suggestions in this chapter have helped many of my clients leave the past behind for a happier future. It's possible that the past provides the perfect excuse not to reach out for the future. When we let go, we risk being vulnerable to different perspectives and maybe even realizing we had it wrong all along. Whatever emotions are tied to your past, they belong with the past. They may seem important. In truth, they are irrelevant because your potential cannot possibly exist behind you.

A 5-STEP PLAN TO LETTING GO OF YOUR PAST

The past should not be thought of as your enemy. Think of your past as your teacher. When you understand where you have been, you have a much better view of where you are going.

Settling your past is an important part of the journey to your Power Seat. You are more prepared than you think to tackle this chapter. Remember, you have already identified your strengths and weaknesses, questioned yourself, and reset your mind. It's now time you clean out some closets and take care of the dirty laundry!

There are five steps in this section that will help you gain the perspective you need to have your best interview yet.

1. Be factual with your feelings.

A fact is an absolute truth. It is unmovable and indisputable. A feeling is an easily moved emotion and/or an emotional state or reaction.

If we are not careful, we give our feelings permission to be treated like facts. I have been deemed an expert at confusing the two many times, so there's no need to feel guilty if you've been accused of doing the same thing.

Each one of us is entitled to our feelings, but not the facts that are established from our feelings. It is important to be honest and accept the fact that your mind doesn't always tell you the truth about your feelings.

I bet you can come up with many examples of ways you convert feelings into facts in your life. Think back to your high school years when you'd stay up well into the night talking to someone—maybe a friend or love interest. The next day, you felt a deep connection to that person and believed you knew him or her better than anyone else. Your mind let you convert your feelings to facts. However, the real facts were that you didn't know that person beyond that one night.

As you look forward, ask yourself if your feelings can be backed up with evidence. Tap into your strengths to change the direction in which your feelings are leading you. Tell yourself you can't afford to be intimidated, bullied, or lied to by your feelings anymore. Not everything you see is what it seems. Not everything you hear is a measurement of truth. Don't assume your feelings deserve to be justified even when your 20% convinces you otherwise.

Of course, not all feelings are bad. Many are legitimate, healthy, and necessary. However, appreciating those kinds of feelings happens the most when you know for a fact you are free from the restraints of the past.

Remember, a fact is an absolute truth. It is unmovable and indisputable. A fact is not subjective and can be proven. Chances are, you have proof in your life to confirm you have been treating your feelings like facts. It is also indisputable that the past is behind you, along with all the feelings that went with it. The time we spend living in the past is the time we will be giving up in the present. Try to be wise with your time, there is no way to get it back once it is gone.

2. Become your own BFF.

It is a rare gift to have a true friend. Lately, my kids come home almost every day with a "best friend" change. Most of the time, it will be a long story involving many tears and much confusion. Friends come and go, but it can be devastating when you lose them.

My Gram used to say, "Christina, in your entire life, you will only have as many true friends as you can count on one hand." The first time she told me this, I thought I had hundreds of friends. Like most kids, I assumed that anyone who wasn't deliberately mean to me could be considered a friend. But, Gram was right. A true friend, one you can count on to stand beside you no matter what, is one of life's rarest gifts.

Our qualifications for a true friend may differ a bit, but it's safe to say we all seek friends who are trustworthy, compass bearing, loyal, faithful, and accurate without variation. They shouldn't be judgmental, but must be steadfast in representing our best interest.

Regardless of who is in your social circle, you must be your own true friend. If you are working against yourself, it will be difficult or even impossible to settle your past. You can't be unsettled and settled at the same time. It is like being hungry and full all at once.

You already have the qualities you need to start being a true friend to yourself. All the qualities you listed in your 80% are exactly the qualities your inner BFF will require. You may not believe that you are equipped, but most likely, you are a true friend to someone already.

If you have ever told a friend not to drive because she had had too much to drink, your advice would be that of a true friend. If you encouraged a friend to persevere after she had worked long and hard to achieve a goal, your motivating words were those of a true friend. If you've let a friend cry on your shoulder and gave the guidance she needed to emerge stronger than ever, you know what it is to be a true friend.

We have all pulled from our resources to uplift, guide, motivate, love, and encourage others. True friends don't want us to fail. They bring out the best in us. Sadly, we often ignore our own cries for encouragement and motivation. By failing to act as true friends to ourselves, we are setting up a tone of failure.

I had a client years ago who was a friend to others but an enemy to herself. In one of our sessions, she was really coming down hard on herself. She told me how she couldn't keep a job because she was a failure at everything. She went on and on, until her phone rang, almost as if it were the period intended for her sentence. As I listened to the conversation, I was amazed at my client's ability to comfort, motivate, and encourage the friend on the other end of the line. Her words were full of kindness, demonstrating true friendship in action.

- "Don't ever say that about yourself. You can do it!"

- "I know you can."

- "Just ask your professor if you can take it again."

- "I totally believe in you."

- "Don't give up."

- "You have worked so hard for this."

- "It's going to be okay."

My client was clearly invested in the success of her friend. I later asked her if she had ever talked to herself the way she just spoke to her friend. She quickly replied, "Seriously? That's what my friends are for!"

It is unreasonable to expect another person to be what you must be for yourself. Like my client, you might believe this is a role for your friends to play. However, waiting for someone else to come along with the right intentions, timing, and patience to encourage, comfort, and uplift you is risky at best.

You will always be vulnerable if you have to rely upon others to tell you what you should be telling yourself. I am not saying we don't need friends in our lives to encourage and help us. My friends are invaluable in so many ways. Every time they catch me holding a grudge, getting angry, feeling discouraged, or acting hurt, they gently and skillfully lead me to my better senses. I appreciate these friendships, but I have a friend within myself that is just as capable.

For years, I was not my own friend. I allowed how I felt about the past to determine what kind of friend I was going to be to myself and others. Since I have been writing this book, I have gained more weight than I care to admit. I know firsthand how hard it can be to struggle with weight loss, so this is quite disappointing. In the past, I would have beat myself up endlessly for succumbing to the temptation of delicious takeout dinners and little to no exercise. Now, I understand that guilt and name calling are counterproductive. Feeling bad about myself does nothing to spur a positive change.

The friendship I have with myself and others has to rely on letting bygones be bygones. I need to look forward to a future that includes kindness and the opportunity for a fresh start. I'm a human being who makes mistakes, but I have the potential to pick myself up and begin again on the right path.

3. Confess.

Confession has been described as a "pillar of mental health" because of its ability to relieve anxiety. Unfortunately, it is rare today to hear people confess anything. Most people view admitting fault as a sign of weakness.

The past can and will take the future right out from under us when given permission to stay. However, by confessing your mistakes and acknowledging your faults, you take away any power the past has over you.

I'm currently working with a young woman who has bravely allowed me to share her story. Sequoia is a beautiful, intelligent, and talented young lady. She has much to offer the world, both personally and professionally.

Originally, Sequoia worked as my assistant. We talked endlessly, shared stories, and exchanged insights. I loved spending time with her, but I had no idea she was suffering greatly on the inside. Sequoia's smile and her youthful energy hid her inner emotional pain.

One day, I received a call informing me that Sequoia had tried to commit suicide. I was shocked and wanted to do everything in my power to help her see how much she had to live for.

During the months to follow, much unfolded about the painful burdens Sequoia was carrying from her past. This is Sequoia's story in her own words:

Nearly three years ago, I was assaulted by someone I trusted. It left me heartbroken, hopeless, angry, and silent. I stopped communicating with everyone, even myself.

The repercussions of my silence were far greater than I ever anticipated, with each crushing feeling building on another until I couldn't tell the truth from a lie anymore. Unfortunately, this became my reality. It was keeping me from being who I should be. I started cutting and then shoplifting before finally trying to slip away forever.

Looking back, I wish I had known the freedom I could have found through confessing the fear and feelings of it all. It turns out the biggest threat was brought on by me. But, as I go forward, I am thankful for the freedom that comes with simply confessing my feelings and fears. In a way, by facing it, I took away all of the power it had over me.

It is super exciting to have experienced firsthand the power of coming clean with my past. Since that point, I have become empowered with the facts and am settled once and for all. I know I will have an interview in my future, and I am happy to say my past will not be a part of it. Until then, I will continue to build on my strengths with the power that comes from admitting the truth under any circumstance.

Sequoia's painful path taught her an invaluable truth. When we confess where we have gone wrong, it enables us to clear the course and start again.

Sequoia is speaking the language of her 80/20. Like the rest of us, Sequoia will always have challenges. The difference is that what she now knows about herself will help her face future challenges with the power of her strengths and the realization of her capabilities.

4. Forgive.

Have you ever stopped to admire the beauty and sound of moving water? It is tranquil and exciting at the same time. But, once the water stops moving, it loses much of its appeal. What once was alive with possibilities is now inert and uninteresting.

I believe every one of us is able to forgive. When we offer others and ourselves forgiveness, it allows us to experience a unique peace and inner strength. How encouraging to know we can find tranquility in the sound of our own forgiveness.

In my life, I have been forgiven at every corner. Without forgiveness, I don't know where I would be. Unfortunately, when I have been the one who needs to do the forgiving, it hasn't always been so easy.

We all know people who won't forgive. My friend Jacob collects resentments like old coins. He even brings them out to compare and share. He moved from town to town, but never found the ideal person worthy of him or his forgiveness. When people attempted to get close to him, they'd eventually make a mistake and he'd shut them out. Jacob interpreted small errors in judgment, such as forgetting an appointment or snapping at someone after a long day, as mistakes that were not worthy of his forgiveness. It did not matter to Jacob if the offending party expressed remorse or tried to change. Once the offense had been committed, Jacob was gone.

Jacob is older now. He spends most of his days reading, watching television and engaging in other solitary pursuits. I have tried to help him see that his unforgiving self has cost him his happiness. Unfortunately, Jacob thinks he is entitled to hold the imperfections of others as justification for his decision not to forgive. I have reminded him that none of us are perfect, and, because of this, we have no business withholding forgiveness from anyone. Sadly, Jacob will not budge from his view. As a result, he leads a lonely life of quiet desperation.

This mindset of "unforgiveness" is certainly a luxury Jacob cannot afford. Truthfully, none of us can. Perhaps my friend needs to see the implications of his own weaknesses. Actually, it wouldn't hurt any of us to know that we are guilty of placing our flaws and weaknesses on others. Until we realize this, we will continue to be harder on others than we have the right to be.

To avoid becoming like Jacob, consider the following:

- Forgiveness doesn't mean you are excusing the other person's actions. You can still forgive someone who is obviously in the wrong.

- To forgive, you don't need to tell the person that he or she is forgiven. Forgiveness that happens only in your heart is just as valid as a public declaration of forgiveness.

- Forgiveness doesn't mean you aren't allowed to have any more feelings about the situation. You can forgive someone and still feel sad about what you have lost.

- Forgiveness doesn't wipe the slate clean. Once you've forgiven someone, there may still be other issues in your relationship that need to be resolved.

- You can forgive someone and make a conscious decision to no longer include them in your life.

Remember, the first act of forgiveness always begins with ourselves. If we are unwilling to let go, we will indeed be keeping ourselves from fulfilling our future potential. By not forgiving the past, we are saying we want to stay in it. We are making it our number one distraction.

The power you apply to your present will largely come from the ability to forgive what happened in your past. Without forgiveness, there will be no growth, no change, and no opportunity for progression.

5. Apologize.

The trappings of the past are dangerous to us in many ways. It is not easy to look at the reflection of our weaknesses. The pain we cause ourselves and at others is bound to leave its mark! However, you CAN get past it if you can get through it.

If you're held up in this section with roadblocks you can't picture getting through, I understand. We are all coming from different places. Don't get discouraged.

Don't be afraid to "settle up" the past with an apology. "I'm sorry" is one of the most powerful phrases in the English language.

An apology is a tool to help you tap into your hidden potential. However, in order for this tool to be effective, your apology must be complete and sincere. An effective apology has five parts:

1. A clear "I'm sorry" statement that specifically acknowledges the offending action.

2. An expression of regret for what happened.

3. An acknowledgment that social norms or personal expectations were violated.

4. An empathy statement acknowledging the full impact of your actions on the other person. (This is the most often overlooked part of an apology, as empathizing with someone who has been hurt makes many of us quite uncomfortable.)

5. A request for forgiveness, as well as an acknowledgment that it may take some time for the recipient to feel emotionally ready to move forward with your relationship.

When you apologize for your mistakes, even the smaller ones, you are refusing to be limited by your imperfections.

POINTS TO REMEMBER

- We all have past hurts and insecurities that lead us to doubt our own abilities. However, the difference between successful people and those still struggling is that successful people have learned to let go of the past. Instead of dwelling on previous disappointments, they make a conscious decision to live in the present.

- To let go of the past, you must:

  - Learn to separate your facts from your feelings. This will allow you to objectively evaluate the situation instead of being swayed by unreliable emotions.

- Start every day with the goal of being your own friend. Be trustworthy, loyal, faithful, and supportive of your own best interests. Avoid passing judgment at all costs.

- Confess your burdens, sharing what mistakes you've made. By confessing past indiscretions, you wipe the slate clean for a better future.

- Forgive others who have done you wrong. Think of forgiveness as a gift for yourself, since forgiving others for their mistakes will free your mind to better focus on your present goals.

- Apologize to those you've hurt, even if your mistakes weren't intentional. Accepting responsibility for your actions shows you're that much closer to taking your Power Seat.

Activity: Forgiveness and Apologies

"We must be willing to let go of the life we've planned,
so as to have the life that is waiting for us." – Joseph Campbell

There are people in your life you can and should forgive. Let's not waste any time dwelling on past disappointments. Forgiveness is a necessary step in escaping the debilitating past. It's also the greatest gift you can give, both to yourself and those who you choose to forgive.

Write a list of those you continue to hold responsible for hurting, upsetting, cheating, or lying to you. Your list might include business associates, family members, neighbors, or former friends.

I need to forgive:

1. _____

2. _____

3. _____

4. _____

5. _____

As you review your list, remember that none of us are perfect. You are most likely on a list or two yourself, even if you didn't really mean the hurtful words you said. As human beings we will make mistakes. The important thing is that when we know better, we do better.

Now, make a list of people you owe an apology to. Your list might include people who are close to you as well as people who were simply in the wrong place when you were having a particularly bad day.

I need to apologize to:

1. _____

2. _____

3. _____

4. _____

5. _____

Finally, don't forget that you must also forgive and apologize to yourself. Below is a list I made for myself. Feel free to add to it or say these aloud daily to help you settle your past:

- "I will try my best to not be held captive in the past."
- "I will try my best to avoid being controlled by my feelings."
- "I will try my best to respect the facts."
- "I will try my best to admit when I am wrong."
- "I will try my best to forgive others and myself."
- "I will try my best to apologize."
- "I will try my best to appreciate my mind."
- "I will try my best not to compromise on what I know."
- "I will try my best to be my best every day."
- "I will try my best to respect myself."
- "I will try my best to look within myself for the answers."
- "I will try my best to check myself daily."
- "I will try my best to know my 80/20 inside and out."

Chapter 5:
Silence Your Inner Enemy

"Very often we are our own worst enemy
as we foolishly build stumbling blocks on the path that leads
to success and happiness." – Louis Binstock

As intelligent as we imagine ourselves to be, many of us are missing the mark on the logical approach to personal success. Astronauts Neil Armstrong and Buzz Aldrin walked on the moon in 1969, but millions of everyday people are still struggling to walk with themselves.

Why does it seem so hard to study who we are and learn how to properly manage, nourish, and motivate ourselves? The answer is that our 20% has endless opportunities to creep in and infect our lives. It becomes our pattern and our problem.

Could it be that we are bored or perhaps we just don't know how to identify with who we are? I don't know about you, but when I lose interest in something, I instantly give up. For example, I once wanted to learn how to knit like my best friend. I purchased yarn, picked out patterns from Pinterest, and diligently tried to master this new skill for about two weeks. Then, I became bored with the project and decided to move on to something else. If I had been honest about my own strengths and weaknesses from the beginning, I would have known that patiently counting stitches and rows wasn't the right choice for me.

Don't settle for less than your best! Defend your strengths! Convict your weaknesses! Justify nothing! Your inner enemy is in your 20%, hiding in your negativity, cynicism, insecurities, and self-seeking purposes. When we look deep into the eye of our inner enemy, we should know the risks and rewards of silencing it. There is always a price to pay when standing for a cause, facing persecution, or going toe-to-toe with a bully. If you know what to expect when you are preparing to silence your troublemaker within, you will be more likely to stay the course and live it out.

This chart may offer some guidance as you're struggling to banish your inner enemy once and for all.

Looking at it from the chart perspective, we understand the enemy's strategy clearly. Your 20% provides the ammunition that your enemy requires to keep your insecurities, imperfections, failings, flaws, and shortcomings at your center. As a result, you are in a cycle of thinking that you need to rely on your weaknesses to cover up and defend your insecurities and imperfections.

Don't feel bad about making this common mistake, but be aware that this cycle is counterproductive to your progress as a healthy communicator. It robs you of the opportunity to be satisfied, content,

Risks = A Powerless Seat	Rewards = A Power Seat
Left out of drama	Days filled with peace and productivity
Excluded from gossip	More time for positive, productive, conversations
Won't have a need to lie	Has fewer burdens to bear
Won't find pleasure in lying	Become honorable and credible
Will have fewer "friends"	Will value quality of friends instead of quantity of friends.
Can't always be right	Won't need to be right to be happy
Will have to put the needs of others first	Secure within oneself and happy to take a backseat
Flaws will become visible to others	Welcome criticism, eager to learn
May not be as popular	Don't need to fit in anymore
People will question new found confidence	No longer a follower, but a steadfast leader
Won't be the star of every situation	Don't need to be validated by others
Won't be able to blame others	Fully responsible for one's own actions
Failure will become more obvious to others	Quick to admit failure, comfortable not being perfect
Forgiveness shows weakness	Forgive easily

authentic, and in the moment. You'll have a hard time thinking about anybody else when you are all wrapped up in providing the enemy with what it needs to keep your attention.

Going back to my earlier example, I should have realized that I was going about trying to master this new skill all wrong. Instead of trying to learn how to knit without any help from others, I should have joined a class where I could tap into my strengths as a gentle, loyal, and compassionate communicator. Learning from others and sharing what I had learned would have been a better way to ensure my success. My inner enemy set me up for failure.

If you've read this far, you believe you have what it takes to strengthen your mind, relationships, and communication skills. Push yourself even further by being on task, focused, and deliberate to allow the best of who you are to surface. With each passing day, you will improve on becoming who you really are. Deciding to make this commitment is great, but to keep it real and relevant requires a daily check and renewal.

STOP LETTING YOUR INNER ENEMY LIE TO YOU

Your inner enemy is an expert at lying to you. By definition, a lie is the deliberate intent to mislead and deceive. A recent study found that most of us lie with astounding regularity. According to a 2011 survey, people in the United States lie 1.65 times a day.

Lying might seem easier than telling the truth, but the long-term consequences aren't worth the short-term gain. It takes but a moment to damage your reputation with a lie and a lifetime to restore it. In the book *Crucial Conversations: Tools for Talking When Stakes Are High*, authors Kerry Patterson, Joseph Grenny, Ron McMillan, and Al Switzler refer to "clever story telling" as a way we try to let ourselves off the hook or release ourselves from responsibility. Let us not go there. We aim to be accountable.

We must educate and train ourselves to be intentional and respectful in keeping the truth. Lying or "creative story telling" seems to be easier and accepted culturally more than ever before. Go against this trend. Lying isn't profitable in your life or in the goal of becoming a dynamite interviewee.

Let's have a moment of truth with our lies:

1. A lie is a noun.

2. A lie always involves a victim.

3. A lie is conceived in your mind.

4. A lie gives birth in your mouth.

5. A lie takes full form in your words.

6. A lie bites the hand that feeds it.

7. A lie lives forever.

8. A lie will always outsmart you.

Some of us are better at telling the truth to others, but we might tell little lies to ourselves. For example: Nobody likes me. I'm worthless and have nothing to offer. I have never done anything wrong. Breaking ourselves from lying habits, whether to ourselves or others, isn't easy, but it can be done. Let yourself celebrate the little victories as you get closer every day to denying your 20% and living out your 80%. Every time you can discipline, manage, and motivate yourself and others, it is truly a victory.

POINTS TO REMEMBER

- Your inner enemy is your 20%. Your negative qualities are constantly creeping in and sabotaging your efforts to manage, nourish, and motivate yourself.

- To be successful, you must always be willing to defend your inner strengths. Give your 80% the attention it deserves so you can strengthen your mind, relationships, and communication skills.

- Your inner enemy can't be trusted. Lies are the tools it uses to mislead and deceive.

Activity: Learning to Face the Truth

"You will face your greatest opposition when you are closest to your biggest miracle." – Shannon L. Alder

I was listening to a talk show the other day where the question was asked, "When meeting the love of your life, would it be a deal breaker if you found out that he could read your mind?"

Think about this carefully. If you knew a person could look at you and know every thought in your head, what would you do? If truthful, I suspect many of us would convince ourselves there are plenty of "fish in the sea" and search for a safer mate.

If we tell ourselves that when we lie, our lies will be exposed, we might become highly motivated to tell the truth. It is a lie that deceives us into thinking that we can be counterfeit and genuine at the same time. We can't produce answers of truth if we are coming from a lie to start with. So then, the truth will be our compass. I hope you allow it to guide you in your pursuit of the Power Seat.

The truth isn't always pleasant, but learning to be honest with yourself is an important part of your goal of owning your interview. To better understand your complicated relationship with the truth, challenge yourself to write honest answers to the following questions:

1. What was your most recent lie?

_____

2. How do you feel when someone lies to you?

_____

3. What lies do you tell yourself? (For example, do you often feel as though nobody likes you or that you're incapable of being successful? As you now know, these negative feelings are lies we tell ourselves!)

_____

4. What negative consequences have you experienced as a result of telling lies?

_____

5. Are you known as a liar among your friends and family?

_____

6. Do you tell lies on instinct or are you a premeditated liar?

_____

7. Would you lie in an interview? Why?

_____

8. Do you lie routinely in your conversations?

_____

9. Do you get caught in your lies? If so, how do you feel when you've been called out for being less than truthful?

_____

If you've discovered you have a problem sticking to the truth, here are three practical suggestions to help keep you honest:

1. Put photos of random eyes up on the walls around your work space or anywhere you spend the majority of your time. It may look strange, but tricking your brain into thinking that someone is watching you will encourage honesty. (If you can't handle the thought of floating eyeballs plastered throughout your office, try redecorating with pictures of people you'd find it difficult to lie to. For example, if your grandmother is a role model who always encouraged you to tell the truth no matter what the consequences, frame an 8 × 10 photo of the two of you together and keep it prominently displayed on your desk.)

2. Write down your thoughts before you speak them. Even if you don't consider yourself to have a way with words, the simple act of writing something down creates accountability. It's hard to lie when there is a traceable record of the truth.

3. Remind yourself beforehand that every time you lie, you become a little less of who you could be.

Activity: Letting Your Inner Beauty Shine Through

"Beauty is not a light in the face. Beauty is a light in the heart."
– Kahlil Gibran

It's been my experience that most women would like to change a few aspects of their physical appearance. Perhaps they shy away from short sleeve shirts because of a little underarm jiggle or they wear only dark colors because they were once told that black takes off 5 pounds.

There's nothing wrong with wanting to look and feel your best, until you start to let insecurity about your physical appearance sabotage your efforts to be a successful communicator. For many years, my client Shelly struggled with the belief that she had nothing to offer because of a noticeable scar across her face. Regardless of what she was doing in her life, she used her scar as a crutch or an excuse to give up on communication.

Shelly got used to her audience cutting her slack or making excuses for her inability to responsibly communicate. In my mind, I believe Shelly carried tremendous guilt because she knew she was capable of much more.

During one of our sessions, I decided to make her scar disappear. I guess my years as a model paid off because I learned from some of the best makeup artists around how to cover up what you don't want the world to see. When I was done with Shelly, you wouldn't know she had a scar. I will never forget watching her stare at her flawless face in the mirror.

After she got over the shock of her disappearing scar, I sat her down for a little chat. I started asking her questions about different scenarios I knew had happened in her life. I asked her to come up with verbal solutions or verbal offerings to present to the other people involved.

Something incredible happened as Shelly wrestled with how she wanted to respond. For once, she was able to focus on the situation and the other individual, and even possibly a solution, rather than on her scar. I could see she wanted desperately to be a contributor and a positive communicative force—she just needed to give herself permission.

Think about your own life. What are some attributes of your physical appearance that make you feel less than confident?

_____

_____

_____

_____

_____

_____

In what ways have you let your insecurity over your appearance act as your inner enemy? For example, have you ever told yourself you didn't deserve a promotion because clients would relate to your "prettier" coworker better?

_____

_____

_____

_____

_____

_____

Brainstorm a list of things you could do to help your inner beauty shine through, giving you the confidence boost you need to be a successful communicator. For example, perhaps you could make an appointment with a professional makeup artist to learn how to cover blemishes or meet with a hairstylist to give you a new look that will let you face the world with confidence.

_____

_____

_____

_____

_____

_____

Think about the women in your life who radiate inner beauty, especially those who don't reflect conventional standards of attractiveness. What qualities do these women possess that make others feel drawn to them?

_____

_____

_____

_____

_____

_____

Chapter 6:
Techniques of Strong Communicators

"Communication—the human connection—is the key to personal and career success." – Paul J. Meyers

I once had a beautiful young client named Rachel who believed the word "F*ck" belonged in every conversation. When she first came to see me, I was completely shocked at how often she used this word. Was she trying to sound cool or edgy?

When I confronted her, she said, "What's the big deal? This word is everywhere, it's on T-shirts, hats, and bumper stickers. Politicians use it. Celebrities use it. Why can't I use it?"

Many people think the F-word is a vocab staple. Truthfully, it has no place on the Power Seat. Nothing can take away from beauty like the sound of ugly. Rachel had stopped respecting both words and herself. She didn't realize when she spoke that she was defining herself with her word choices. Rachel needed to identify the kind of person she was meant to be so she could choose a communication style that was in line with her true strengths.

When she came back for her next session, I asked Rachel to watch a video I'd found on the Internet that featured gang members showing off their strangely similar f*ck-laden communication style. Then, I had her write down three people she most respected and asked her to imagine any of them using the F-word in conversation as the gang members just had.

Fortunately, Rachel quickly realized that her strengths and her communication style were mismatched. It took some effort on her part, but she eventually learned to be consistent with respecting words and herself. Today, Rachel is a dedicated elementary school teacher who is a positive role model for her students.

YOUR WORDS DEFINE YOU

When you speak, keep in mind that what you say will be defining you. Mean what you say. Say what you mean. Resist the urge to engage in negative dialogue. It will take self-control and practice to reverse bad speech habits, but the results will be worthwhile.

FOCUS ON FACTS, NOT FEELINGS

Most of us determine how we communicate based on how others make us feel. This is one of the most common ways we stumble into bad habits and patterns. We look to others to determine what we do and say. We even let them decide how we say it.

It is not uncommon for my clients to cry in a session. It can be emotional when you are slaying the dragon within. However, my former client Denise catered to her emotions 24-7. After an interview experience where she broke down in tears and excused herself from the room, she decided to come see me.

As we sat down to get to know each other, Denise cried at least four different times. She filtered everything through feelings until her feelings had become her facts. It is hard to be logical or effective when you are emotionally charged. Since feelings can change instantly and frequently, they tend to be distracting.

Denise kept up with her sessions with me and started focusing on where the facts lived within her. Her homework was to identify 100 facts in life and 100 feelings as well.

For her facts, Denise listed items such as,

- Barack Obama is the first African-American President of the United States.

- It takes 8 minutes and 17 seconds for light to travel from the sun's surface to the earth.

- Alfred Nobel invented dynamite in 1866.

- There are 60,000 miles of blood vessels in the human body.

For her feelings, she listed:

- France is the best vacation destination.

- James Bond is the best character ever.

- The color blue makes you calm.

- Fifty is old.

After Denise established a healthy understanding of the difference between feelings and facts, she was able to analyze her communication style. She realized that she had been adopting feelings and making them factual.

By doing this, she was communicating from a defensive position. Denise spent most of her time analyzing everybody's motives. This makes it very difficult to offer the best of yourself to anybody when you think you always need to defend yourself.

Today, Denise is now a stable and healthy communicator. Let her story show you why putting so much emphasis on our feelings is dangerous.

THE MORE YOU TALK, THE LESS VALUABLE IT BECOMES

Do you tend to talk until you're forced to listen? Let's reverse that. Try listening until you have to talk! The legendary actor John Wayne was great at this. He was always making the most of his words—never wasting an opportunity to be powerful in his speech. When asked how he was so effective as an actor, he replied, "I talk low, slow, and say little." I believe if he were to expand on that he might say, "The more you talk, the less valuable it becomes."

Of course, John Wayne had script writers to direct him with every scene. However, the basic concept still stands. Who's to say we can't utilize every scene in our own lives to be as dynamic as possible?

Excellent communication is illustrated by others who have been in the spotlight, like Ronald Reagan, the actor turned President of the United States. Reagan was known as the *great communicator*. He was simple, clear, and sincere in his speaking patterns. His strong leadership was in large part because he communicated with style and a personal belief in what he was saying. Reagan never let us see him sweat. He had a beautiful harmony, pitch, and pace while balancing composure and personality effortlessly. His standards were high and uncompromising, which was faithfully reflected in his thoughts and words.

7 ESSENTIAL STAPLES TO HELP YOU CLAIM THE POWER SEAT

Now that we've identified some strong communicators, it's time to practice adopting their techniques. What follows are seven key words designed to bring you closer to the Power Seat: Respect, Penetrate, Engage, Interest, Visualize, Organize, and Teach.

As you work on developing these techniques, consider the example of actress Téa Leoni's character Elizabeth Faulkner McCord on the TV series *Madam Secretary*. She is a fabulous example of a powerfully authentic communicator. Elizabeth is always using her best self and the knowledge she has of her strengths to guide her. She brings an offering to every conversation, empowering those around her. She has strong, decisive leadership skills that are respected because she is aligned with an honorable motive of being true to herself, which is always evident and present in her communication. The result of her interactions leave others inspired, encouraged, and motivated to be better.

1. Respect

Respect focuses on caring for the identity and value of another person. In conversation, respect works like an invisible boundary. Respect blocks you from unnecessary insults, interruptions, innuendoes, contradictions, and other conversational mishaps. Who do you respect? How do you communicate with that person? I would bet there is an awareness, politeness, and attention to detail with every word. Imagine if you applied that same attitude to every conversation. Sometimes we feel that it is not necessary to go out of our way for everyone. We convince ourselves that the circumstances just don't warrant our respect. If we tell ourselves a certain person does not deserve respect, we are lowering our inner standards. It's like saying we are only gracious communicators when we want to be.

The Power Seat communicator is steadfast under pressure and will not be easily moved by unfavorable circumstances. It is easy to be on your best conversational behavior when you like, admire, or want something from the other person. We have all had those premeditated, manipulating, and dishonest exchanges. However, we are not better for having them. The respect you carry for yourself and your integrity to uphold it needs to be the main ingredient in every one of your conversations. When your focus is on your character strengths and bringing them to life through your thoughts and words, all your conversations will be respectful. Respect is given as well as earned. Strive to be worthy of both at all times!

2. Penetrate

When you can penetrate through to your listener you will be remembered. The ability to speak and be heard is one thing, but the ability to speak and be remembered is another. Every effective communicator has the ability to be remembered. It is not so much because of the eloquent way in which they speak, but in the way they deliver their message. There is an old saying, "It's not what you say, but how you say it." This is only half the truth; the other half is that you must mean what you say and say what you mean.

The art of breaking through depends on the truth in you. The truth shall set you free and declare you memorable every time. You may not be the most popular, but you will penetrate through to your audience with your authenticity every time!

History has many great examples of men and women who left a mark, struck a chord, and rattled a cage because of their ability to penetrate their audience with a powerful message. You don't have to be addressing the nation to be powerful, passionate, and memorable. You just have to know, believe, and trust in what you are saying. You must be uncompromised and authentic. When you're willing to stand and deliver on your truth, you can rest assured you have made a lasting impression on your listener.

3. Engage

Engage your listeners, and they will thank you! How well do you attract and involve your listeners? It is harder than it seems to keep people's interest and attention because there are so many distractions in the modern world. Smartphones and other technology give people a way to "check out" even when they are physically in the room with you.

Since you can only control your part in the conversation, give it your all! Having the ability to connect with another during conversation requires awareness, eye contact, and plenty of "bounce passes" (asking questions/seeking other opinions)! As humans, we love the sound of our own names. Maybe this has happened to you once or twice while you are in a conversation, lecture, or meeting: You start to lose focus, then all of a sudden, you hear your name, which brings you right back to attention! Use the power of the name to keep your audience engaged. While you are talking, casually make sure to remind your listener that you know their name.

4. Interest

Interest is the hallmark of any great conversationalist. They will always ask questions, having a genuine interest in you, your life, and your well-being. When we find people interesting, it is because they are unique, which means they are living a life authentic and free from the influence of culture.

It is refreshing to converse with a person who has interests, hobbies, and adventures to share instead of small talk or gossip. Set a goal to be interested and interesting in life. Conversation can get selfish, petty, redundant, and stagnant without constant reminders to avoid it.

I once read a funny, but true, comment about modern day conversation in *Readers Digest*. It said, "The hard thing is that interesting people never want to talk about themselves, and boring people never want to ask questions."

Finding a point of interest in the person you are speaking with, such as a characteristic, trait, curiosity, appreciation, concern, or commonality, awakens levels of alertness in you and shifts the focus off you toward them. It happens often that we lose interest, so be prepared to have some practical application to use in a pinch. The Power Seat communicator must not be afraid to be interested or be too shy to be interesting. Set yourself apart by working to become an interested and interesting communicator.

5. Visualize

Visualize yourself being an incredibly effective communicator. Most of us have had moments of visualization at one point or another. It usually catches us off guard and happens by chance. We may visualize wants like houses, vacations, or dream cars to temporarily feed our cravings. However, we rarely tap into the power of visualiza-tion to inspire, motivate, and push us toward achieving goals and creating change.

Thai Nguyen is the author of *5 Ways to Manifest Your Reality with the Power of Visualization*. He does a great job of providing practical, powerful, and effective ways to use visualization for positive change. One of the areas Nguyen writes about is how to live as if you have succeeded in your goal. This means you should dress, talk, look, and act like the person you want to be. When you do so, you are essentially seeing, believing, and belonging before arriving.

Whether you think you can or you think you can't, you are correct in your assumptions. Visualize your way to success.

6. Organize

Think back to your high school English class. When you were asked to write an essay, you were probably instructed to make an outline demonstrating your plan for the beginning, middle, and end. In the beginning, you included a "hook" to grab the audience's attention. In the middle, you included your most substantive points. In the end, you reviewed what you had said and created a call to action.

By taking the time to plan what you want to say, you will be able to avoid boring your audience or forgetting to include key facts. The same principle applies to your interviews. It is important to organize your thoughts and outline your key points to keep your conversation on track.

It is also important to declutter your inner-view message. When you can assemble an organized and easy to understand presentation about who you are, you will be without a doubt effective in the Power Seat.

7. Teach

In order to take the Power Seat, one must be able to present their inner–view, as an expert would, in a way that others can easily comprehend and learn from.

I remember having to take a speech class in school. There would always be different topics that I would have to understand, organize, and present. I remember that my first couple times in front of the class I presented my subject with very little believability. Later, my teacher told me I was presenting from the posture of a student. If I wanted to be convincing and persuasive, I would have to present with the mindset of a teacher.

Have you ever tried pretending that you are teaching the subject you are trying to learn? If not, try this approach. It is often helpful to adopt a teacher's mindset in order to identify confidently with the subject you are studying or presenting.

If you have ever gone into a classroom with the idea that you are going to learn only to have a teacher that does not know how to teach, it is disappointing. It wouldn't matter if they were unprepared about the subject or they just didn't have the confidence to share what they knew effectively, you would still be let down.

This is how your interviewer will feel if you fail to educate him or her on the subject of you. Telling yourself that you are the teacher in the room will help you step into the Power Seat role with an established tone of leadership. Believe me, there will be no one better qualified for this position in your interview than you.

EXPANDING YOUR POWER SEAT KNOWLEDGE

An effective communicator employs several tools to get her message across. I like to think of these tools as ways to expand your Power Seat knowledge.

1. Composure + Personality.

There is a time and place in every conversation where you must have a balance of understanding. For instance, a serious conversation that requires deeper thought and complex delivery would suggest that a calm, self-controlled, poised answer would be more appropriate. Then, there are other times when the cheerful characteristics of your unique personality play a role in the energy and direction of the conversation. One must realize when there is a time for composure and a time when personality is called for. When you use both in balance, it is a very useful communicative tool.

Don't be afraid to let your unique personality shine through, however. Instead of trying to be what you think the other person wants, stay true to your own unique attributes. Regardless of whether you are being composed or a bit more lighthearted, trust your strengths to fulfill your purpose. When you come across as authentic, kind, and approachable, people will be eager to hear what you have to say.

2. Cut the fat.

Another aspect of speaking effectively has to do with your fat content. This doesn't mean your literal BMI status. I am referring to the fat that is in your words. I'm sure you've had conversations with people that talk a lot and say nothing.

When you start every sentence with "yeah" or "well," you're adding empty calories that take up space. This leaves your audience unsatisfied.

Years ago, my family and I were out having dinner at a restaurant. This was my chance to order the steak I had been craving for weeks. When it came, it was mostly fat. I left the restaurant unsatisfied. Remember this metaphor when you speak. Fill your conversation with the good stuff. We want to leave our listeners with the steak itself, not the fat.

Imagine if you were given only ten minutes to talk to your family and then you would have to wait an entire year before speaking to them again. I bet you would choose your words wisely and deliver only the meat of the steak.

When we deliver fatty words, the listener has to cut through them and likely goes away disappointed. We need to consider the value of words in order to regain our respect for them. Take what you know about yourself and use it responsibly to improve your proficiency in communication. If you want to be a positive and productive conversationalist, you can be. It is entirely up to you.

3. Keep pace.

Pace yourself when you speak. Have you ever had a conversation with a person who talked so fast you had no idea what he or she was saying? How about a person who talked so slow that you forgot most of what was said? Pace is extremely important when you are attempting to hold someone's attention while communicating a point.

Many people think they must fill every moment with words or the situation will be awkward. As a result, they rush through their thoughts and trip all over themselves trying to fill space. They end up disrupting the pace, losing composure, slipping out of the moment, and forgetting to listen.

The give and take of conversation is like a beautiful dance. It's the back and forth that supports balance and comprehension. One cannot achieve this balanced harmony in conversation if they are not in the moment.

When you think of pace, consider taking what I call *beats* or *pauses* as you change thoughts or take turns talking. This will also help you avoid accidentally cutting people off when they are speaking.

4. Use voice inflection to your advantage.

Think about the last time you read a story to a child. Did you change your voice to match the different characters? Did your voice get higher as something exciting was about to happen? Did you whisper during the quiet parts of the story?

Changes in voice inflection can be used to communicate emotion as well as to help hold a listener's interest. To improve your inflection in an interview situation, smile and take long, slow, deep breaths. This helps to loosen your vocal cords, bring your pitch down, and convey a general impression of friendliness.

5. Color your words.

Color your language to set yourself apart from the crowd. Years ago, I was working with a client on her interview skills. This young lady had a monotone voice with no variation in range, pitch, or expression. While she was sharing exciting, informative facts and insights, they had little impact for the listener. I kept thinking how I could help her when, one day, a beautiful rainbow sprawled across the sky. I was captivated by its color variation, and a light went on in my head. The next time we worked together, we found a picture of a rainbow. I asked her to speak the sound of each color. Matching her voice to the different colors worked and started a trend with my clients in learning how to color their words.

Try writing down a variety of different colors. For example: **RED**, GreEn, YeLLow, **O**range, Bla**CK**. Now, try saying each word in a different tone. Try matching your tone to what you would imagine the color would sound like. Then repeat over and over again. Once you get the hang of it, try incorporating some of those different tones with the words you use to communicate.

6. Utilize the power of three.

Adding *facts, statistics,* or *quotes* to your presentation is an excellent way to support your key points while keeping audience interest high. Look for relevant facts and statistics from recent news stories or set up Google alerts for useful tidbits from your specific industry.

You may also want to consider keeping a small notebook to jot down quotes from people you admire, so you can incorporate them into your communication when appropriate. Quotes support your position in much the same way as facts but add an element of human interest to your presentation.

Representing the true facts of who you are establishes you as an expert. However, adding quotes, stats, and facts to your available resources supports your authoritative position in the Power Seat.

7. Make eye contact.

When you make eye contact with someone, you come across as friendly, confident, and engaged. But many of us fail to make eye contact as often as necessary due to shyness or a tendency to let our minds wander when socializing.

If you find eye contact intimidating, try practicing with a trusted friend or family member to increase your level of eye contact in everyday situations. Be patient with yourself, as it takes time to break bad habits.

They say the eyes tell the story. I think there is a lot of truth to that. Regardless, make sure that your unique inner self comes out through your eyes. Use your eyes, and know that they can work wonders for you. Keep in mind that shifty eyes or eyes that tend to look up in the sky or down to the ground can give off a false impression that you are nervous or untrustworthy.

If you are interested in learning more about body language, one of my judges when I competed in Miss USA was Dr. Lillian Glass. She has written several books that cover the topics of body language and how to read people. These would be great additional resources to check into if you're looking to improve your skills in this area.

8. Offer perspective.

Years ago, I took a Dale Carnegie course based on the book *How to Win Friends and Influence People.* I learned a great deal in that time, but perhaps one of the most effective tools was to speak *with* a person and not at a person. When talking with a person, you engage on the same level to demonstrate an awareness of their presence and value. Subconsciously, this relaxes your audience. It plants a seed of authenticity and approachability in the conversation.

In any conversation, your goal should be to offer your own perspective while remaining open to the other party's point of view. Can you accept that your opinion is not the only opinion? If you can, that is good news. Every effective communicator understands the importance of taking into account other possibilities and opinions outside their own.

I am not suggesting you try to appeal to every viewpoint. Rather, I'm asking you to graft within your opinion the presence of perspective. This does three things:

1. It disarms the listener, which means they will be more willing to listen instead of discredit your idea while you are sharing it.

2. The listener will likely give your opinion consideration.

3. You create an opportunity for honest, open, and productive dialogue. Never hesitate to give your listener permission to disagree with you. Half the battle in persuading others is giving them respect by acknowledging their credibility.

9. Stay in the moment.

Julie came to me wanting to perfect her interview skills. For years, she had been struggling with what I call *internal stuttering*. Her speech was fine to the casual observer, but on the inside she was tripping all over her thoughts and doubting them as fast as she was having them. Because Julie spent her energy trying to please and impress, she lost her confidence in her own voice.

Julie had been trying to climb the corporate ladder with little success. As we worked through our sessions, Julie started to understand that there isn't room in a moment for both greatness and doubt.

One thing we did to help Julie stay in the moment was to ask her to write what she wanted to say as she was saying it. This exercise helped her to re-train her brain to not jump ahead or lag behind. Julie also had to act out or attempt to sign every word she spoke, much like she was playing a game of charades. This created a harmonious union between her thoughts and her words. Today, Julie is one of the best communicators I know.

Staying in the moment with your message communicates that you are focused, fearless, and uninhibited. When you're in the moment, there's no time to become anxious or second guess what you will say. As an interviewee, this is a wonderful way to keep fear and anxiety out of the conversation.

10. Listen, think, and then speak.

Most people struggle with this concept. It takes discipline, focus, and trust to slow yourself and your conversation down. We often multitask in life and the way we communicate. However, if you practice this technique, it will allow you to be a better listener.

When you listen, think, and then speak, you will pick up on important and perhaps subtle insights from the conversation. It will take practice not to think about what your response should be while the other person is talking. Expect that you will have to trust yourself and let go of a little control. Believe that you will come up with the authentic, accurate, and truthful response in due time.

I promise you that when you give yourself a chance to listen, you will not be disappointed in how wide and deep your thoughts can go. Since you've slowed the game down to listen, you will have set the stage to speak knowledgeably.

Truthfully, there is much we say that it is unnecessary. There are many times we don't really answer the question or address the real issue. This is simply because we get ahead of ourselves and our conversations.

In an interview, the most important thing we can do, next to being authentic of course, is to use our time wisely so those evaluating us can get the most accurate impression of who we are. As you train yourself to listen, think, and then speak, you will become a much more effective conversationalist and interviewee.

POINTS TO REMEMBER

- There are seven essential staples that will help you claim the Power Seat:

  1. **Respect**—Show genuine care for the identity and value of another person.

  2. **Penetrate**—Penetrate through to your audience with your authenticity.

  3. **Engage**—Use awareness, eye contact, and plenty of bounce passes to engage your listener.

4. **Interest**—Ask questions, showing a genuine interest in the other person's life, activities, and overall well-being.

5. **Visualize**—Visualize yourself being the best communicator you know.

6. **Organize**—Organize your thoughts to keep on track and avoid boring your listener.

7. **Teach**—Assume the mindset of a teacher to reflect the fact that you're an authority on the subject of yourself.

- Expand your knowledge with Power Seat tools you can use to add a little pizzazz to your communication. They'll help ensure that your audience is hanging on your every word.

  1. Composure + Personality

  2. Cut the fat

  3. Keep pace

  4. Use voice inflection to your advantage

  5. Color your words

  6. Utilize the power of three

  7. Make eye contact

  8. Offer perspective

  9. Stay in the moment

  10. Listen, think, and then speak

Activity: The 10-Day Challenge

"The art of communication is not for the talented BUT rather for the educated." – Christina Nepstad

Change can be scary, but making meaningful improvements in your life will be easier if you break your goal down into smaller and more manageable parts. When you commit to success, you will achieve it!

In this activity, I want you to apply only the one technique that is recommended for each day. Don't get ahead of yourself. The steps may seem simple, but they take a concentrated effort to properly master. Focus on doing the best you can with each day's challenge.

At the end of the challenge, think about which day was easiest for you and which day was the most difficult. Try to brainstorm strategies you can use to work on accentuating your strengths and minimizing your weaknesses. For example, if you're a generous and compassionate person who finds it difficult to smile and make eye contact because you are shy, try to reframe these activities as simply another way to show encouragement to others. When you approach life through the lens of your 80%, there's no limit to what you can accomplish.

On the 10 challenges below, write down the techniques, circumstances, and lessons you learned from implementing each of these exercises. It is also worthwhile to record any actions or reactions that may have happened because of your concentrated effort to become a masterful communicator.

Day 1—LISTEN. Your challenge today is to listen actively! Listening may be awkward for you, but you are fully capable of doing it. Believe in yourself and tell your mind who's in charge. You will be offering a great gift to those you encounter. Everyone wants to be heard.

_____

_____

_____

_____

_____

Day 2—GIVE SINCERE COMPLIMENTS. Today, your goal is to sincerely compliment every person you talk with. Keep it honest. It can be quite rewarding knowing that your kind words have made someone's day. If it seems unnatural, you need more practice. It will become second nature before long.

_____

_____

_____

_____

_____

Day 3—USE WARM, INVITING BODY LANGUAGE. Your challenge today is to begin all of your conversations with warm, inviting body language. A two-handed handshake is a wonderful approach. Other options include a pat on the back, a hug, or a gentle touch to the forearm. Bring your listeners in. Provide them a place of importance with your greeting.

Try not to cross your arms as it can indicate that you are unreceptive or unenthusiastic. Try leaning in slightly as you listen intently. This will give the other person an indication that you are interested in what they have to say. Above all, never underestimate the power of a smile!

_____

_____

_____

_____

_____

Day 4—AVOID GOSSIP. Stay away from gossip of any kind. You will find yourself both refreshed and shocked by the amount of time you've previously wasted on disruptive, empty, and nonproductive conversations.

_____

_____

_____

_____

_____

Day 5—OFFER ENCOURAGEMENT. Make an effort to offer some form of encouragement in every conversation. Not everyone will be looking for encouragement, but you are still capable of offering kind, compassionate, and motivating words. We can find our greatest source of encouragement right within our 80%.

_____

_____

_____

_____

_____

Day 6—SMILE. Greet everyone you meet with a smile, even if you're not feeling particularly happy at the moment. I have witnessed people offering up smiles under the worst of circumstances. Their positive attitude soon spreads to others around them.

_____

_____

_____

_____

_____

Day 7—CUT THE FAT. Your challenge today is to cut the fat from your chat. As you speak with people throughout your day, eliminate your filler words. Many times we don't even know that this has become a habit in our speech pattern, but it's vital that you strive to be aware of the fat content in your conversations. Remember, knowledge is power!

_____

_____

_____

_____

_____

Day 8—MAKE EYE CONTACT. If you have ever tried to have a conversation with someone who is easily distracted and constantly looking around, you know how annoying this can be. Your goal for today is to keep your eyes focused on the person you are speaking with. This is a simple way to leave them feeling like they are the most important person to you in that moment.

_____

_____

_____

_____

_____

Day 9—BE INQUISITIVE. Your challenge today is to be inquisitive. With every conversation, plan to learn something about every person you meet. Pretend you are Lois Lane, the intrepid newspaper reporter. Ask the key questions any journalist would: Who, What, When, Where, Why, and How. When you are learning about others, you are most likely talking less about yourself. Sometimes, that is a good thing!

_____

_____

_____

_____

_____

THE POWER SEAT

Day 10—KEEP YOUR PACE. It is very distracting and ineffective to speed or stall through a conversation. A smooth and steady pace makes it possible for your audience to follow along. If you are invested in the moment, this should help you stay on cue.

_____

_____

_____

_____

_____

Chapter 7:
Planning for a Bright
"Inner View" Future

Seeing your future starts with a vision, a decision, and a plan. Our future is everything in front of us. Our past is everything behind us. However, the way in which we live our present will determine our future!

Strive to leave the past behind you as you plan for a brighter future. With your 80% leading the way, you can't go wrong.

THE VISION IS THE BRIDGE
Many people use visualization to see their plan for the future come

full circle. Close your eyes and see yourself drinking from the fountain of your 80%. In the same fashion, imagine a soundproof, escape-proof holding tank where you will keep your 20% captive. Visualize yourself as a great communicator, doing your part to create and sustain healthy relationships.

Make this a habit, closing your eyes and setting the scene for powerful progress in your attitude. See your Power Seat and hear yourself speaking in strength.

When using visualization as a bridge to achieve your visionary plans, you might consider the story of Gerald Chertavian to inspire you. In 1985, he began serving as a Big Brother through the Big Brothers Big Sisters mentoring program. He was deeply touched by the struggles of the boy he was mentoring, a 10-year-old who was living in a neighborhood known for its crime and drug use. Gerald was convinced that if the young boy only had the opportunity, he could be just as successful as his peers from more affluent neighborhoods. "I thought it was so wrong that the opportunities he had access to in life could be limited due to things like his zip code, the color of his skin, the bank balance of his mother, or the school system he attended," Gerald said. "We are wasting so much talent in this country."

Gerald knew that many young people were struggling to do their best in situations just as difficult as the one his Little Brother was facing. He had a vision of a non-profit organization that would offer opportunity where there would normally be none. As a result, he founded Year Up in 2000. This one-year education and professional job training program gives low-income young adults from urban areas a chance to obtain hands-on skill development, corporate internships, and college credits.

Studies have found that Year Up graduates earn 30% more than similar young people who did not participate in the program. An impressive 85% of graduates are employed or attending college full-time within four months of completing the Year Up program.

The first time I heard Gerald speak about his organization, I remember thinking how passionate, convicted, and determined he was when he talked of his vision. It is a fundamental truth that a vision takes passion to be viewed in high definition. Year Up is now hugely impactful across the country—changing the lives of the young people it serves in a way that will create a ripple effect for generations to come.

If you believe in your vision, make a decision and implement a plan. Life is waiting, full of opportunities for you to show off your best self.

A DECISION ALWAYS BEGINS WITH A MINDSET OF DECISIVE ACTION

Your mind will set the course for your success. When you've identified your goal, begin with a mindset of decisive action that helps provide the support system and accountability you need to be successful.

When my friend Maureen decided she would run a marathon for the first time, she set herself up to succeed with a support system to back up her decision. She was smart enough to know that she could easily be persuaded to change her mind. After all, fear and intimidation are working full time in your 20%.

By signing up, paying the money, and telling her friends and family, Maureen was intentionally setting up accountability and support for her decision. She wasted no time in coming up with a written plan, including daily training routines to keep her decision on track.

As time passed, my friend became passionate about reaching her goal. Maureen was smart; she put in place the necessary framework for a training program which would prepare her to run a marathon successfully. As she grew closer to completing her plan, her passion continued to grow. It's not surprising she finished the marathon with a time that beat her initial expectations!

A decision left on its own runs the risk of failing without reinforcement. We easily give up, feel defeated, and court failure if we are not armed with strength, knowledge, and determination.

A PLAN ROLLS OUT THROUGH DEDICATION, KNOWLEDGE, AND DISCIPLINE

Creating a workable plan to reach your goals requires dedication, knowledge, and discipline. Life is unpredictable, and there will undoubtedly be obstacles thrown in your path as you work toward reaching your goal. You must prepare yourself by understanding the risks and having the discipline to face these challenges when they occur.

Years ago, my husband had a plan to ride his bike around the state of Montana. He was planning on raising money for the Boys & Girls Club of America by riding 1,650 in 21 days around the state on a bike.

He did what everyone needs to do when trying to execute a plan for such an ambitious goal. He posted copies of his plan everywhere so he would always be reminded of what needed to be done. He discussed his goal with friends and family to create accountability. He anticipated obstacles by making lists of drivers to follow, campsites to sleep in, safe routes to take, and preparations to ensure he'd have enough food to eat. When he set out on his journey, he was confident that he'd be successful even if he had a flat tire, found a road that was unexpectedly closed, or the weather failed to cooperate for a day or two.

The plan worked for my husband because he also knew to weave his best self into his plan. He made no excuses and was dedicated to reaching his goal. His 80% had to be integrated throughout every detail of the plan in order to make it happen.

It is easy to slip into old habits of trusting our 20% to tell us the plan can't work or simply sabotage it for us altogether. A good plan should have a beginning, middle, and an end. Your dedication to the entire process is critical to your plan's overall success. Go for it! You can own your plan and make it happen!

POINTS TO REMEMBER

- Let your 80% lead the way as you create your vision and plan for the future.

- Visualization can be a powerful tool for creating a brighter tomorrow. Close your eyes and picture your goal in as much detail as possible. See yourself drinking from the fountain of your 80% as your 20% is held captive and powerless.

- When you have a plan, set up a system for accountability and support. This decisive action greatly improves your chance of success. It's easy to give up and feel defeated when you don't have the necessary systems in place to put your plan into action.

- Dedication, knowledge, and discipline are essential to any plan, whether you're trying to master a new hobby or get a promotion at work. Don't fall back into the habit of letting your 20% sabotage your efforts.

Activity: The Relationship between Your Present and Your Future

"Your present circumstances don't determine where you can go;
they merely determine where you start." – Nido Qubein

Our attitude about our decision, vision, and plan is very important for our Power Seat interview, but equally so is our outlook on life itself.

Our lives are constantly changing, but the choices we make today can set the groundwork for a brighter tomorrow. For example, you could choose to enroll in a leadership training course to gain the skills needed to be a stronger candidate for a promotion. Or, you could let go of past insecurities about your abilities and finally start searching for jobs in the industry you've always dreamed of working in.

As long as you have hope for the future, there's no limit to what you can accomplish. Explore the relationship between the present and your future by taking some time to think about answering the following questions:

What does your life mean to you?

_____

_____

_____

_____

_____

What has been your proudest accomplishment to date?

_____

_____

_____

_____

_____

What would be a good plan of accountability for you?

_____

_____

_____

_____

_____

Think of someone you admire who has had a vision, decision, or a plan to help them achieve their goals. What can you learn from them?

_____

_____

_____

_____

_____

Think of someone you know who has not achieved their goal for one reason or another. What can you learn from them?

_____

_____

_____

_____

_____

Chapter 8:
Case Study—Nikki Learns to Stop Being Trapped in Her 20%

"Weakness of attitude becomes weakness of character."
– Albert Einstein

Nikki was one of the most difficult clients to help. She was a middle-aged professional who had developed patterns in which she found comfort in her weakness. She was under the control of her bad habits. She was impatient, intolerant, judgmental, relentless, unyielding, and rude. Nikki's judgment and criticism echoed off the walls. Everyone in her company was a target.

Unfortunately, Nikki learned early on that her weaknesses gained her attention. Every jab that gained her personal status and momentum was motivating. She quickly fell into a pattern of relying on her weaknesses to manipulate those around her.

Nikki came to see me because her life was falling apart both personally and professionally. She had been demoted at her job, and her position was at risk. As far as her communication skills went, people ran the other way when they saw her coming. Nikki told me she once said to herself, "People will do anything they can to avoid a conversation with me." Nikki finally did realize that destructive patterns are simply unsustainable.

Nikki was a classic case of a woman trapped in her weaknesses. We spent weeks sifting through the wreckage of her life and relationships. Slowly, she was able to see the pattern of destruction in her life. Nikki realized that she was uncomfortable being vulnerable and scared of being taken advantage of. To cope with her fear and anxiety, she created a barrier of protection through her harsh character traits.

Nikki became reliant on her weaknesses to bring her attention. It was negative attention, but she still craved it nonetheless. Nikki learned that her weaknesses would always deliver a punch and often help her get what she thought she wanted.

Sometimes, we get addicted to the characteristics that create drama and give us a false sense of our own importance. I asked Nikki to describe the difference between a giver and a taker; this is relevant because we must have a clear grasp of what brings power to our lives and our interviews. Nikki was able to break it down and finally reveal to herself that she was in the habit of taking. It is easier than we know to listen, think, and speak as a taker.

Influenced by weakness, Nikki craved what takers often have: a position of importance, attention, and a sense of worthiness. The good news is she recognized she was going about it the wrong way.

We are never more significant than when we are giving. The Power Seat interview is first and foremost an offering. Think of it as a contribution, donation, or a gift. Empowerment is never more appealing than when it is under the authority of our strengths. This is when power becomes remarkable, noteworthy, and momentous.

Sometimes we have to break before we can rebuild. Nikki went on to study a new side of herself and found that being vulnerable really isn't that bad. She learned how to trust her strengths and became fluent in them. Her marriage and health improved. People stopped running from her in the streets and started seeking out an honest dialogue. Six months later, Nikki was promoted to a better position than the one she had been released from months before.

NIKKI'S PERFORMANCE REVIEW: BEFORE

Before Nikki came to me, she would have presented herself in an interview as a taker who was being led by her weaknesses. She allowed others to see her as prideful, defensive, judgmental, and emotional. I imagine her performance evaluation would go something like this.

Interviewer: "Nikki, we want to promote you, but we can't justify it."

Nikki: "Are you serious? I am doing my job to the best of my ability. What more do you want from me?"

Interviewer: "At our company, we place a high priority on mentoring and training junior employees with the potential to advance to upper level management positions. Can you give us an example of how you've served as mentor for your direct reports?"

Nikki: "To be honest, I've been quite disappointed with the performance of my staff. I'm a very busy woman and don't have time to reach out to provide extra help to employees who are still struggling to meet the minimum objectives I have set for them."

Interviewer: "We have had several complaints about your leadership style. Can you tell us what a leader should act like?"

Nikki: "I don't know about other people, but I expect my team to perform at their highest level. Like a good leader, I come down on them when they don't deliver. I tell them what to do and how to do it. If they can't figure it out after that, they should find another job."

Interviewer: "The morale of your team is down. What is the reason for this?"

Nikki: "I would think it is obvious. They are underperforming and feeling the effects of their failure to meet the objectives I have set for them."

Interviewer: "Would you be willing to go through some additional leadership training?"

Nikki: "I appreciate it, but I hardly have the time. Besides, I don't know how that could help the people who need it most, my direct reports!"

Interviewer: "We think it is better to redefine your position for a bit. Do you have any thoughts about this?"

Nikki: "Yes, I feel this is unfair. I don't understand why I should be penalized for the poor performance of others. I am very qualified for this position and think you will be making a mistake. I would hope you would reconsider."

NIKKI'S PERFORMANCE REVIEW: AFTER

After working with Nikki to help her develop a better understanding of how to think and speak from her strengths, the difference in her interviewing style was remarkable. Her answers showcased her intelligence, responsibility, determination, gratitude, and leadership skills. Consider how Nikki approached the following questions after her Power Seat training.

Interviewer: "Nikki, we want to promote you, but we can't justify it."

Nikki: "I understand. May we discuss why you are having reservations about my qualifications?"

Interviewer: "At our company, we place a high priority on mentoring and training junior employees with the potential to advance to upper level management positions. Can you give us an example of how you've served as a mentor for your direct reports?"

Nikki: "I have been a direct beneficiary of many kind mentors throughout my career. I would like to think that I am an approachable person, but I realize that there is room for improvement in this area. I welcome your input regarding ways I could serve as a more effective mentor for our company's junior employees."

Interviewer: "We have had several complaints about your leadership style. Can you tell us what a leader should act like?"

Nikki: "Certainly, but first, I want you to know I am deeply concerned to hear I have disappointed people with my leadership choices. My goal has always been to be a leader people want to follow. I think a leader should ultimately generate inspiration, enthusiasm, and results. I would appreciate the opportunity to regroup and adjust my approach. I truly believe I can be a more positive leader that others will be excited to follow."

Interviewer: "The morale of your team is down. What is the reason for this?"

Nikki: "As the leader of my team, I take full responsibility. The lack of confidence and enthusiasm you see is a reflection of the tone I have set as their leader. I know I am capable of stronger, more positive leadership."

Interviewer: "Would you be willing to go through some additional leadership training?"

Nikki: "That is a wonderful offer. I am busy but will make the time to be there. I know being a leader is a huge responsibility, and I take that seriously. I look forward to learning from those who are the experts in leadership."

Interviewer: "We think it is better to redefine your position for a bit. Do you have any thoughts about this?"

Nikki: "I respect your decision. Yet, would you consider a grace period before reassigning my position? I believe I have the capacity to translate vision into reality. I would also greatly value the chance to reestablish myself as a good and faithful leader."

POINTS TO REMEMBER

- Letting your 20% have a voice means you are passing up the chance to be effective, meaningful, profound, responsible, productive, and memorably powerful. You may be successful in the short term, but eventually you will face consequences similar to those that Nikki struggled with. In an interview situation, you must learn to think and speak from your strengths to be successful. Let your 80% lead the way.

- We are all seeking a position of importance, attention, and a sense of worthiness. However, when you go about fulfilling these goals by leading with your 20%, you're being a taker. To claim the Power Seat, you must develop the mindset of a giver. Your weaknesses may trick you into thinking that you are less powerful without them doing the dirty work. Don't be fooled. You will never be more ineffective than when you are listening to your inner enemy.

- The Power Seat interview is first and foremost an offering. Keep in mind your goal in the Power Seat is to be fully knowledgeable and authentic. As you offer your strengths, you will in turn educate and empower others with the best of who you are. Remember that empowerment is never more appealing then when it is under the authority of our strengths.

Activity: Giving Credit Where Credit Is Due

*"You would be surprised how much can get done
when you don't care who gets the credit." – Ronald Reagan*

You would be surprised how you can keep your listeners engaged when you give them credit! Don't hold back your appreciation and acknowledgments from your listener; it will always be welcome and serves as a useful tool when in the Power Seat.

Here are some examples of simple ways you can credit others for your accomplishments instead of developing a reputation as a taker:

- James, I wanted to thank you for the wonderful quote you gave me the other day. It was exactly what I needed to finish my presentation.

- Kim, I understand you had some great advice for the city on trash awareness. Great job!

- Elizabeth, thank you so much for helping me to proofread my annual report. I appreciate your input and would be happy to return the favor as needed.

- Mark, I just wanted to let you know that I really enjoyed your presentation at Monday's staff meeting. I plan to implement some of your suggestions regarding effective social media marketing early next week. Thank you for your wonderful ideas!

In an interview situation, here are some examples of how you can give credit to others:

- Thank you for reading over my résumé. Few people pay as much attention to detail as you do.

- I really appreciate the advice you gave me. I will work hard to apply that in my life and in my next job.

- There are many that have contributed throughout my career. I must give them credit for helping me grow and mature into this position.

It's a win-win to dish out sincere credit and acknowledgment when possible. Everyone loves to feel appreciated!

Over the next week, challenge yourself to give credit to at least one person per day. Jot down what you said, how that person reacted, and how you felt after you acknowledged the contributions of others.

1. Monday

_____

_____

2. Tuesday

_____

_____

3. Wednesday

_____

_____

4. Thursday

_____

_____

5. Friday

_____

_____

6. Saturday

_____

_____

7. Sunday

_____

_____

Chapter 9:
Case Study—Diane Learns
to Settle Her Past

"Yesterday is not ours to recover, but tomorrow is ours to win or lose."
– Lyndon B. Johnson

Diane was a psychology major with a promising future until one day changed her life forever. She went out for a jog and was beaten and raped.

After the attack, Diane struggled to get back on track. Her physical injuries healed fairly quickly, but the emotional scars lingered. Haunted by insecurity, shame, and self-doubt, Diane dropped out of school, lost touch with her friends, started doing drugs, piled up debt, became homeless, got pregnant, and dated a man who beat her.

Diane lived as a permanent victim, trapped within herself, until our paths met 23 years after that horrible night. She was missing some front teeth, her skin was weathered, her clothes were tattered, and she walked with a limp. As we started to speak, I noticed she stuttered and had trouble making eye contact.

Over the next couple months, however, I would grow to admire this woman for her ability not to judge me as privileged or hate me for having an "easier" life. Diane had suffered for years, and the furthest thing on her mind was to compare the two of us. Despite her struggles, Diane did not wish her burdens upon anyone else.

What happened was nothing short of amazing. She showed up every week like clockwork. She was determined to know what she might salvage of herself. We started from scratch, searching every nook and cranny to find the good, the bad, and the ugly. Nothing was spared. We brought everything to the surface, and what a surprise it was!

Diane's ultimate goal was to interview for a job she saw in the paper. She had not worked in the past decade. We went through all kinds of exercises together, but the turning point for Diane was when she was challenged to find the good that came out of every bad situation. For instance, her relationship with the abusive boyfriend brought Diane a daughter who is now the light of her life. When she was homeless, she realized she was resourceful and compassionate after she helped two fellow homeless people get off the streets. Even going back to her attack, she managed to find good in the midst of unspeakable horror. She SURVIVED!

This exercise helped Diane understand that she can be better instead of bitter. When Diane created her own PowerPoint report on the benefits of unfortunate suffering, she found she was fortunate to be alive, healthy, and able to start over each day. This changed her entire perspective by giving her the closure she needed to reinvent herself.

We spent many more sessions identifying, defining, and proving her many strengths. Diane's passion for victims has led her to be an advocate for many without a voice. She has joined arms with the weak and brought comfort and hope where there was none.

When Diane interviewed for her first job in ten years, she nailed it! Today, Diane thrives as both a person and a communicator. She has positively and gratefully put her past aside so she can focus on living in the moment.

DIANE'S JOB INTERVIEW: BEFORE

The past has a habit of showing up in our lives, including in our interviews. We may not even notice it at first, but it doesn't take much for it to creep in and distract and penetrate our mind, especially if it is a feeling or memory from the past we have left unresolved. We never know what could come up from the past to threaten and distract us.

Here's an example of how Diane would have answered some common job interview questions before her Power Seat training, speaking from the weaknesses of appearing insecure, self-consumed, and defeated.

Interviewer: "Diane, please tell us about yourself."

Diane: "Well, I have been through a lot. I am a victim of abuse and other things. I am trying to cope. I think by getting this job it will help me with my confidence. I also have been out of work for a long time so I really need this opportunity."

Interviewer: "What skills do you have that we can count on?"

Diane: "Hmmm, I have had to be resourceful a lot in my life. When I was homeless, I had to survive with nothing. I was even able to help people under those circumstances. I also was able to pull myself off drugs with a lot of determination."

Interviewer: "How would you handle a disagreement with another employee?"

Diane: "I don't know. I mean I seem to have my share of arguments. It's amazing how people want to take advantage of others. I would just have to follow my gut and survival instincts."

Interviewer: "How many hours can you work a week?"

Diane: "Whatever I need to work to get benefits. I need some dental work and have some new health issues I need to take care of."

Interviewer: "Would you be OK starting at our lowest entry job considering you don't have any experience?"

Diane: "Not really. I have spent my life as a victim, which has forced me to give up a lot, almost everything, actually. I might not have the experience, but I can learn fast. I have watched life pass me by and am tired of it, to be honest."

DIANE'S JOB INTERVIEW: AFTER

We all have certain feelings, emotions, memories, and scars that are not in any way easy to deal with or settle. However, the steps we covered earlier in the Settle Your Past chapter are extremely effective helping to clear the air, lighten the load, bridge the gap, ease the pain, and, most importantly, reconcile past.

Take a look at how Diane learned to effectively interview after going through these steps to deal with her own past trauma. Notice how she's speaking from her strengths of being hard-working, logical, determined, honest, resilient, and resourceful.

Interviewer: "Diane, please tell us about yourself."

Diane: "I would love to share what makes me unique. Life has taught me a great deal about myself. I will say that I am prepared for this opportunity because I am organized, focused, steady, and determined to make a positive difference."

Interviewer: "What skills do you have that we can count on?"

Diane: "You can count on me to approach each day determined, resourceful, flexible, and resilient. In addition, I am aspiring to become an expert in typing, cold calling, and route management. I am enrolled in online courses and reading several books on developing my skill set in these areas."

Interviewer: "How would you handle a disagreement with another employee?"

Diane: "It is not realistic to think disagreements will never happen. However, I am grateful to have learned the best way to handle a disagreement is to respect the other person's perspective. When I disagree with someone, I try to listen to their perspective and brainstorm a solution that we can both agree on. I believe compromise is essential in developing any mutually respectful relationship."

Interviewer: "How many hours can you work a week?"

Diane: "I gave that a great deal of thought before applying. Based on the fact that I want to succeed at this job and I would welcome the chance to receive benefits, I am looking forward to a full time position."

Interviewer: "Would you be OK starting at our lowest entry job considering you don't have any experience?"

Diane: "Yes, and I truly appreciate the offer. However, I would be extremely grateful if you would evaluate the quality of my work as I go and consider me for advancement when your confidence level is raised. My goal is to prove to you I am worth the investment."

POINTS TO REMEMBER

- Before you can claim the Power Seat, you must settle your past. Even if you're the victim of a traumatic assault like Diane, you must find a way to move forward. If you don't, you run the risk of allowing your past to rob you of your future opportunities.

- Once you've reconciled your past, you're in a place where you can see how adversity has made you stronger. Think of yourself as bamboo. You may bend, but you are not broken.

- In an interview situation, you don't need to go into detail about the challenges you've faced in the past. Your past does not define who you are today. Focus on communicating how adversity has helped you better understand your 80%. Strive to be better, not bitter.

Activity: Out of Sight, Out of Mind

"Some of us think holding on makes us strong,
but sometimes it is letting go." – Herman Hesse

Diane's story shows that any obstacle can be overcome with the right attitude. However, don't make the mistake of thinking your past doesn't need settling if you've never been through a trauma of the same magnitude. Here are some examples of smaller ways in which your past might interfere with your present:

- You were fired from your last position and feel convinced you're being unfairly persecuted as you seek new employment.

- You're self-conscious about the fact that you don't have the same level of formal education as many of your peers. Even though you're confident you could handle the job requirements, you hold yourself back because you're missing the right degree.

- You've been discriminated against in the past based on your age, race, gender, and/or socio-economic status. As a result, you walk into an interview situation feeling like a victim instead of someone who is ready to claim the Power Seat.

- You're seeking lower paying positions out of financial necessity but feel angry because you know you're worth more.

- You have always wanted to be a stay–at–home mom and you feel resentful because you need to seek employment in order to support your family.

Settle your past by creating a list of previous hurts that are negatively affecting your interviewing process. Write them down in as much detail as you want. Venting is completely appropriate for this activity, even if you've already forgiven the offender as part of your Chapter 4 exercise. When you're finished, rip the letter into a million tiny pieces or burn it in your fireplace. Physically letting go of the past in this manner will free your mind to move forward.

Chapter 10:
Case Study—Jessica Learns
to Set Her Mind

"What the mind can conceive and believe, and the heart desires, you can achieve." – Norman Vincent Peale

Jessica came to work with me after losing at her second attempt to win the Mrs. California pageant. When we sat down for our first session, I quickly learned she had a small speech impediment and suffered from Multiple Sclerosis. Yet, her genuine presence and strong resolve made these facts irrelevant. You could tell she was comfortable in her own skin and in the moment with her thought process. This sure sign of authenticity is a must for anyone seeking to assume the Power Seat.

As our sessions progressed, it became clear that Jessica relied on the strength of her mind more than most. Knowing that her body was often weak, she would depend on her mind to coach her through. However, her mind was not doing its job at the Mrs. California event.

I asked Jessica to recount how she felt when she was interviewing at the pageant. She described feeling inadequate, scared, and powerless to be heard for who she really was. What Jessica described made sense. These were the classic symptoms of mindless mischief.

We decided to map out all the other areas of Jessica's life to try to pinpoint when her mind was being naughty, disobedient, and under-purposed. We split her life into three sections: mental, physical, and social. Then we listed the related activity, attitude, and overall impact of her approach within each section.

This exercise helped Jessica to see how often her mind cooperated. As a mom, she was effective, accurate, and trustworthy—even though being a parent is many times unpredictable. Jessica was an active volunteer in the community and served on many committees where she was able to offer up with confidence her ideas, strengths, and services. She was also working toward being a volunteer ski patrol rescuer when she was diagnosed with MS. This was something completely new and challenging. But, because she had already appointed her mind to the task, she found the inspiration to continue toward reaching that goal.

What was happening with Jessica's mind in her interview? Why was this amazingly accomplished woman with an active and obviously strong mind feeling weak and insecure in her interview? Many of my clients at first are convinced that they can only be confident and powerful in situations where they have been validated previously. However, that is simply not the case. We can look at Jessica's examples and believe that her mind was indeed set for success even within the unpredictability of many unknown conditions.

Through our exercises, Jessica proved to herself that the common thread in her success was the input of her mind. When she set its course with a prescription of purpose and value, it would eagerly rise to the challenge. Her mind was capable of providing her focus, resources, and confidence.

Jessica went on to win Mrs. California and to this day credits her mind for leading the way.

JESSICA'S PAGEANT INTERVIEW: BEFORE

In her interviews prior to coming to The Power Seat program, Jessica was feeling inadequate and powerless to be heard for who she was because she was allowing the interviewers and the circumstances of the interview itself to determine how she would respond.

Without the enlisting of her mind, Jessica might have answered the following questions this way.

Interviewer: "What do you expect to gain by competing in pageantry?"

Jessica: "I enjoy pageants and hope to put the prize money toward my child's college education."

Interviewer: "Why do you want to be Mrs. California?"

Jessica: "I want to be Mrs. California because I like the program, and I think I would be a good representative."

Interviewer: "What can those who will be working with you during the year (if you win) expect from you?"

Jessica: "Others can expect me to be willing and excited to do the job. I also hope I can show them that they can trust me to be a great representative and a hard worker."

Interviewer: "How will you manage your time as Mrs. California with the demands of a family?"

Jessica: "I will make sure my family understands that this commitment is for a short year, and they will need to adjust."

Interviewer: "What could be controversial about you?"

Jessica: "Oh, I don't think anything about me is controversial. I am a very easy going and agreeable person."

Interviewer: "How will you make an impact on others as Mrs. California?"

Jessica: "I would love to make an impact by just being me. I really enjoy people and love talking to people. I feel confident that I can make a positive impact."

JESSICA'S PAGEANT INTERVIEW: AFTER

When Jessica felt like she was afraid to be too much of who she really was, she stopped trusting her greatest resource—her mind. Once she learned how to avoid the common trap of feeling like she needed to be someone other than herself to please or gain approval from others, her interviewing skills improved dramatically.

Interviewer: "What do you expect to gain by competing in pageantry?"

Jessica: "I hope to develop a better understanding of myself while gaining an opportunity to share my experiences as a wife and mother living with a chronic illness. My hope is that I can use my story to better educate the public about the challenges of life with Multiple Sclerosis."

Interviewer: "Why do you want to be Mrs. California?"

Jessica: "That is a great question. I have had three goals since I got married. All of them involve challenging my personal growth. I have realized that I am the best version of myself when I am serving others. This position is a great opportunity to do just that."

Interviewer: "What can those who will be working with you during the year (if you win) expect from you?"

Jessica: "I'm glad you asked. I can guarantee they will not receive perfection. However, they can fully expect a woman who is loyal, dedicated, resourceful, determined, humorous, often hungry, and a great listener."

Interviewer: "How will you manage your time as Mrs. California with the demands of a family?"

Jessica: "Anybody that has a family understands that finding balance can be nothing short of a magic trick. Therefore, I will rely heavily on my common sense, organizational skills, and consider what is realistic and fair to both my family and this position."

Interviewer: "What could be controversial about you?"

Jessica: "Controversial, as we all know, is often a euphemism for interesting and intelligent. With that said, I can tell you I am passionate, empathetic, and tireless for the underdog, underprivileged, and unloved. Unfortunately, in today's world, this is often considered controversial."

Interviewer: "How will you make an impact on others as Mrs. California?"

Jessica: "I often tell my kids that if they want to influence someone and impact their life, they need to make sure they are living up to the best of who they can be. Therefore, I believe the same is true for me."

POINTS TO REMEMBER

- Authenticity is a must for anyone seeking the Power Seat.

- If you suffer from interview anxiety, there's a good chance your mind is being naughty, disobedient, and under-purposed. Your

20% is working against you, hiding the wonderful qualities of your 80%.

- The common thread of success is the input of your mind. Challenge yourself to look for examples of how you set a goal and diligently worked to achieve it. Refer to these examples whenever you're feeling nervous about an important interview.

Activity: Banish Mindless Mischief

*"Failure will never overtake me if my determination
to succeed is strong enough." – Og Mandino*

Jessica took home the crown because she learned how to put a stop to the mindless mischief that was sabotaging her efforts to claim the Power Seat. Even if you have no interest in entering the pageant circuit, the lessons she learned can help you become a more effective communicator. Don't let your 20% work against you!

List at least three accomplishments you're proud of in each section of your life:

Mental

1. _____

2. _____

3. _____

Physical

1. _____

2. _____

3. _____

Social

1. _____

2. _____

3. _____

After you've made your list, examine your attitude and the overall impact of your approach toward reaching each goal. For example, if one of your accomplishments in the physical section was training to run your first 5K, think about how you planned to reach your goal. Did you create support and accountability by getting a workout buddy and posting updates on your progress via social media? Claiming the Power Seat is an incredible accomplishment. Brainstorm strategies you can use to enlist the support of your mind, then place your list in your daily planner or another spot where you can refer to it as needed. Aim to purposefully aspire to what you desire, my friends. You ARE capable of what you believe you can achieve.

_____

_____

_____

_____

_____

_____

_____

_____

Even though it may seem like these accomplishments are unrelated to interviewing effectively, they are all connected. Success, regardless of the form it takes, is all about hard work, planning, and determination. With the support of your mind, anything is possible!

Please answer these interview questions to the best of your ability now that you have completed your Power Seat training.

"What can you offer this company?"

_____

"How have you learned from a mistake you've made in your past?"

_____

"Why would others want to follow your leadership?"

_____

"What aspects of your personality fit best with this particular opportunity?"

_____

"Why do you want this job?"

_____

"What are your greatest professional strengths?"

_____

You did it! I would be willing to bet that you answered these same questions a bit differently now. Let's refer back to the beginning and compare your answers. The goal is to successfully express your individuality and honesty through the power of your unique strengths.

Congratulations!

You did it! You were able to uncover the power, productivity, creativity, capability, and confidence that live within an authentic you! Now that you recognize your own voice, please don't ever ignore it. What good would it be to locate a long-lost friend and then turn down the chance to reunite?

From this point forward you will be empowered and equipped with a new understanding of yourself that will enable you to own the Power Seat anytime, anywhere! It is an honor and high calling to live true to your potential and new found strengths.

It is time to get excited about your future interviews. Each and every one of them is an opportunity for you to shine and make a positive difference in the lives of others.

I want to leave you with one last word of encouragement. For those days when your strengths seem miles away, for those moments you can't find your true voice, remind yourself you are only human. Perfection is unobtainable and certainly not the Power Seat way.

If you can embrace that truth for yourself, you will forever be trading in the good for the great.

Love,
Your Power Seat Coach

Appendix:
Additional Resources

Are you eager to learn more about how you can be a communicator worthy of the Power Seat? The following are some of my favorite websites and books that help reinforce key Power Seat principles.

Toastmasters International
https://www.toastmasters.org
Toastmasters International is a nonprofit organization that operates clubs dedicated to helping members improve their communication, public speaking, and leadership skills. Consider finding a location near you to practice using voice inflection, eye contact, pace, and other Powers Seat techniques of communication.

Bartlett's Familiar Quotations

http://www.bartlettsquotes.com/

Bartlett's Familiar Quotations has been the top source of entertaining and informative quotes for over 100 years. Now, you can visit the book's website and download a convenient app that lets you search for relevant quotes from your phone or NOOK.

TED Talks

https://www.ted.com/talks

Sometimes the best way to learn to be a strong communicator is to study the techniques of compelling speakers. Browse through the various TED talks archived online to see how the featured speakers use Power Seat Techniques to hold the audience's attention. Jot down any interesting facts you learn to use in your next interview.

Dale Carnegie Leadership Training

http://www.dalecarnegie.com

If you're able to do so, I'd highly recommend enrolling in one of the Dale Carnegie leadership courses based on his popular book *How to Win Friends and Influence People*. These courses provide hands-on training in the art of clear communication, leadership, and personal development.

Dr. Lillian Glass

http://www.drlillianglass.com

Dr. Lillian Glass, renowned human behavior and body language expert, is the author of multiple books of interest to those seeking to claim the Power Seat—including *Toxic People, The Body Language of Liars, He Says She Says, I Know What You're Thinking, Attracting Terrific People,* and *Say It Right.*

Crucial Conversations:
Tools for Talking When Stakes Are High
By Kerry Patterson, Joseph Grenny, Ron McMillan, and Al Switzler
As the cofounders of VitalSmarts, a corporate training resource, the authors share their tips on how to prepare for high-stakes situations and transform anger or hurt feelings into powerful dialogue. This book is a must-have addition to your library if you want to learn to be persuasive, not abrasive.

Getting Past Your Past:
Finding Freedom from the Pain of Regret
By Susan Wilkinson
This book discusses six steps to help you let go of regrets, including learning to forego secrets, live authentically, and grieve for your old dreams. It's written for a Christian audience, but the lessons still apply regardless of your particular spiritual beliefs.

Emotional Intelligence 2.0
By Travis Bradberry and Jean Greaves
It's no secret that emotional intelligence is crucial to your success, but many people fail to realize that you can work on increasing your emotional intelligence over time. Learn how to use the four core EQ skills- self-awareness, self-management, social awareness, and relationship management–to achieve your fullest potential.

Just Listen: Discover the Secret to Getting Through to Absolutely Anyone
By Mark Goulston

If you've ever felt like no one is listening to what you have to say, this book is for you. *Just Listen* describes simple techniques that can promote productive communication in any situation, including how to use empathy jolts to bridge communication gaps and how to subtly calm an angry or aggressive person.

CPSIA information can be obtained
at www.ICGtesting.com
Printed in the USA
FSHW01n0711110518
48124FS

9 780692 562352